Creative Techniques in Photo-journalism

Creative Techniques in Photo-journalism

Terry Fincher

Lippincott & Crowell, Publishers *New York*

CREATIVE TECHNIQUES IN PHOTO-
JOURNALISM

Copyright © 1980 by Terry Fincher.

First published 1980 in Great Britain.
All rights reserved. Printed in Great Britain
by The Anchor Press Ltd. and bound by
William Brendon & Son Ltd. both of Tiptree,
Essex. No part of this book may be used or
reproduced in any manner whatsoever
without written permission, except in the
case of brief quotations embodied in critical
articles and reviews. For information address
Lippincott & Crowell Company, 521 Fifth
Avenue, New York, N.Y. 10017.

FIRST AMERICAN EDITION
Published by arrangement of B.T. Batsford Ltd,
4 Fitzhardinge Street, London W1H 0AH

U.S. Library of Congress Cataloging in
Publication Data
Fincher, Terry
 Creative techniques in photo-journalism
 Includes index.
 1. Photography, Journalistic. I. Title.
TR820.F52 1980   778.9′907   79–25315

ISBN 0–690–01899–1

79 80 81 82 93 10 9 8 7 6 5 4 3 2 1

Contents_____

Acknowledgments_____

My acknowledgments go back a long way, right to the time I first started photography – for that's really when this book began.

The training I received in my early days, although very basic, set me in good stead all the way through my career. Fortunately, I learned the hard way as a boy in the developing room what a good photographic print was all about, and for that my thanks are due to the late Tom Bunt who, in my opinion, was the greatest Press printer of all times: he worked with what today we would consider primitive equipment and yet turned out quality prints, many of them daily. Others I'd like to thank are people like Harry Doors, Jim Parfitt and John Stean, who all worked for the Keystone Press Agency; they taught me many aspects of the picture business, including a very important one, that of getting the names and facts in my captions right – and I've done my best here. I'd also like to acknowledge my first picture editor on a daily newspaper, Len Hickman of the *Daily Herald* – he knew and felt pictures. Two other picture editors I also worked with – it must have been the greatest picture team ever in Fleet Street – Frank Spooner and Gerry Cook, both of the *Daily Express*; these three men moulded my life sending me around the world on major assignments.

I would also thank my wife, June, who has sat up late at night transcribing my tapes and notes that I had previously recorded or written in some of the world's remote places, from Rhodesia to North America. Many thanks to daughter Jayne (today also in the picture business), who helped get the pictures together for this book.

I A Personal View

Press photography is, today, a very fashionable profession. It has regained a respectability that it once held in its infant days. I am not, of course, referring to the modern Paparazzi type of photographer who uses more brawn than brain. It is the hard-working press photographer I refer to, whose work fills the pages of newspapers and magazines alike. Yes, at last my side of photography, i.e. Press photography, has lost its Andy Capp image – that of a man in a scruffy raincoat, running at the heels of a reporter.

For what reason the press photographer was pushed down the ladder for so many years, I just don't know. After all, it was his pictures that graphically told the story then, and can today bring back ways of life now gone. As the old saying goes: 'One photograph is as good as a thousand words'.

I do admit that I have fears of losing our new-found respectability, for there is an element amongst us who seem to have no pride in the profession. They treat it as just an ordinary, uninteresting job. This is not so and never will be. We are privileged people seeing history in the making, meeting the people who make it, and there are times when thousands of eyes can be watching us working. So let us conduct ourselves in the right manner.

Personally, I'm very proud of being a Press photographer. It's an élite club. Today we are titled photo-journalists: a rather snobbish name I feel – too much journalist and not enough photographer. Then again, we do have to identify ourselves with the type of photography that we are doing, which is in fact reporting with pictures.

A photo-journalist should be able to cover the whole spectrum of photography, taking it all in his stride; from fashion to sport, from news to features. One thing I am grateful for is that the photograph can't be misquoted as often as the written word. There are, of course, occasions when pictures are used out of context – it could be for propaganda purposes or sensationalism – but on average the good news or feature picture appears in its true light as taken by the photographer.

Like everything of today, things are not the same as a few years ago. The press photographers of that time are as far removed from those of today as is the old 5 x 4 Speed Graphic from a modern 35mm camera. The press photographer of yesteryear – I am talking about my younger days – would carry a dozen double-dart slides, giving him 24 exposures. The camera was fitted with a lens of about 5 inch focal length, which would give very little depth of focus. If he was lucky he might have a range-finder that worked. Nevertheless, he got his pictures sharp, even if he did pace out the distance from camera to subject every now and again. The slower plates or films used did nothing to help but, looking back at the pictures taken then, they had a charm of that period, a moment in time caught forever.

Today, in contrast, one camera bag holds many rolls of 35mm film, which enables him to make hundreds of exposures in black and white, or colour. In the same bag he carries several camera bodies with different lenses, which gives him great mobility and variety. How times have changed!

The Press photographer of yesteryear still has one thing in common with his modern counterpart: the picture editors still want the one great picture that sums it all up. As we say in the profession, the 'Block Buster'.

With the passing of the big picture magazines the need has returned for the photographer who can capture a complete story in as few pictures as possible, which then can be used as a major spread in a newspaper. A picture that is different and contains impact does just that. There is little space for the long-winded picture stories in the magazine and newspaper world of today – television does it much better. Television is a fierce competitor of the newspaper. The moving colour picture complete with sound that's transmitted from remote parts of the world arrives in our homes at the same instant; what is shown on TV in the evening news bulletin one day, can make the following morning's newspaper pictures in black and white look prehistoric.

Fortunately, newspaper men are canny people. The use of intelligent layout, a good caption story and a catchy headline gives something more than television. The reader can always study a newspaper at his leisure, keeping it for posterity or just for reference. The same yardstick applies to the colour magazine; printed several weeks later, it is pointless unless there is that something different to entertain.

I suppose a photo-journalist could call himself an entertainer, for entertain he does. Millions of people look at his work each day, on early morning buses and trains, in hospitals and homes. He takes them out of their everyday life as they study his pictures, whatever the news, tragedy or joy.

For those wanting to make a profession of photo-journalism, be warned. It's hard. Many give up and move into other fields of photography. For those determined to make it – or even those who have made it – I will try to give some guidance which, I might add, is purely my own personal view. I will say this – I don't know a photographer who knows it all. We learn a little each day. No two assignments are the same; even the hardy chestnuts like Wimbledon tennis or the Epsom Derby always provide that something different.

In today's world of photo-journalism we have to be creative. I am not talking about contriving; I'm talking about creating with a capital 'C'. You create opportunities, create impact in your photography and create quality in your work; only then do you create success.

I believe strongly in the still picture, much more than I do the movie. The movie cameraman is a part of a team. To my way of thinking, the photo-journalist is a complete individual much more than someone working in any other form of photography. Even when working with a reporter, you remain an individual. In those moments before you take a picture, you think, 'Correct exposure?', 'Am I in the right place?', or about other small technicalities – so many things can go wrong. Finally comes the press of the button that will record for ever a really great picture.

It's the photographer's final decision, his know-how, his confidence, plus an element of luck, that's important. A reporter can always re-write; the photographer on a 'hard news' assignment is not offered this luxury. There have been times that I have travelled thousands of miles and waited days to take a photograph that was all over in a 250th of a second.

One piece of advice I would like to offer would-be photo-journalists. I quote the late Sir William Conner, better known as 'Cassandra' of the *Daily Mirror*, in a piece he contributed to a book called *Fleet Street*:

'So, young stranger, my advice is don't come near us. Don't come on in "for the water's warm". It's not, it's hot. It's also freezing cold and it's rough too. But it is the best, the finest, the most furious, the most exciting bath of life that anybody could ever take.

But, for Gawd's sake, mind the old plug 'ole.'

I am asked, many times, where one starts in my field of photography. To be honest, it's a difficult question to answer. Unlike doctors, lawyers or engineers, who attend their respective places of learning, there are unfortunately very few and limited facilities for photo-journalists; the world is our university. Of course there are photographic colleges which provide courses on the technical side of photography. These, I might add, do an excellent job, turning out yearly hundreds of photographers who will be successful in the many different fields of photography.

A very limited number of photo-journalists will make it. Maybe I'm sticking my neck out with this statement, but possibly not more than ten each year will reach their final objective. I think this is due to one important fact – the hard unofficial apprenticeship one must serve. There is also the need for many personal qualities, such as having a little of the doctor, lawyer and engineer, plus stamina, determination and courage. Many of my colleagues do and I respect them for it; that is why they are successful. that is why they are successful.

It is impossible for photographic colleges to teach the nitty-gritty of everyday life but, as I said before, they can and do perform an excellent job of technical training. It will be the photographers themselves who finally develop a maturity that enables them to tackle the assignment in hand.

Many of them do come into our side of the profession late in life, and are very successful. Personally, I think one should start at an early age if possible. I started with the Keystone Press Agency at the age of fourteen as a Fleet Street messenger boy, then into the darkrooms and finally out with a camera at the age of twenty. Many other photographers also started at Keystone in the same way and later became famous. At the same time I am not saying we should all leave school at fourteen – education is a must in this sophisticated world.

Then again, fundamental and practical experience is important. How do you gain this experience? Do you go to a photographic college, or work in a dark-room with a News Agency? You must first learn the basics. No photographer is going to achieve the ultimate results without the understanding and feeling of darkroom work. Unfortunately, the standards of many darkrooms vary from first class to appalling. Still, the ambitious individual will over-come this.

There is the other side of photo-journalism, that is the journalistic feel for the story or the approach to it – where do you start here? Once again the most sensible way is to start at the bottom, with either a local newspaper or news agency, gaining journalistic and photographic experience at the same time if possible. You will then hopefully soon break down the barriers that all who seek success must break down, before your future is assured. I have deliberately restricted the photographs and text of this book to what I consider to be my everyday photography.

It is not a book about award-winning pictures or my photographs over the years; it is intended to give some idea of what we as photographic journalists should be able to produce, of what our work involves, of my feelings and what is expected of us. The photographs are taken only over the past ten years and if not on equipment that is the same, then equipment similar to that which I use today. My photography has matured in this period but the basic style itself is, I think, more or less the same. Although I no longer work for a large daily news-paper, my photographic needs have been replaced by a more international demand for my work.

The needs of most daily newspapers are for 95% monochrome and maybe 5% colour. Over the past few years I have been concentrating on colour, which now takes up over 80% of my work. It is because of these changes that my work has been given a broader scope. Leaving aside the actual technical side of picture taking, the technique and thought behind a picture in both black and white and colour is, I think, pretty much the same, and I hope the pictures in this book and some of my thoughts will help you to understand the photo-journalist that little bit more.

2 Good Picture Taking

Taking a good photograph is something that should come easily to the experienced photo-journalist, provided the material is there to be photographed, even though it might mean some concentration and observation. Events that are difficult to photograph are a particular challenge, and those of us who are able to pull a good picture out of the bag on these 'nothing' stories know the great feeling of satisfaction one has afterwards.

In general, most pictures are there for the keen-eyed. On a news story the photographer will be using a combination of luck, ability and technique to produce his end result. The luck comes in the form of being in the right place at the right time, but luck needs a little help at times, so you should try and help your luck by thinking ahead as events are happening. For example, an experienced photographer covering a major motor-racing event will know where the best possible vantage point is – the most likely place where an accident might happen, where to be on the first lap when cars are bunched up. If it is a Grand Prix and points are vital for one driver to clinch a world championship, what time should a photographer allow himself to get back to the pits for the final scenes? It is no good being at the back of an excited crowd, unable to get through. It is this sort of thinking that I'm talking about. A photographer covering a demonstration where demonstrators are clashing with police or troops should never, if possible, get himself into a position where he is unable to photograph events because he has to take cover or gets himself arrested. On these types of stories a photographer should definitely always be thinking and watching, but it applies to most stories, from war to sport.

Your ability and technique comes from long experience of taking pictures, knowing how to use your equipment to its best advantage. Use the wrong lens at the wrong time and you might as well have stayed at home. In exposing your film there is a little more leeway for mistakes; here the darkroom can help at times, with extended developing or whatever may be needed. But while all the hustle and bustle has been taking place I hope you have concentrated on the focus. Getting pictures sharp comes difficult to many, even when aided by the fast film and lenses of today. Photographers are still getting pictures out of focus, mainly through not concentrating as a result of nervousness. On the most hair-raising story, try to keep your mind calm; do this by thinking technically – it keeps you from becoming a bundle of nerves. Just concentrating a little on the technical side helps you to do things automatically. In glamour and fashion photography you rely more on technique and ability. Here, there is no luck. Your technique is in the lighting, your ability in the posing and creation of the picture, though of course it is helped tremendously by having a good model! Good feature-type pictures often come out of the hard news story, such as a disaster or war. These pictures are captured by the photographer with the compassion and ability to see what others don't, to produce a high quality photograph that has impact. This type of picture will be used on its merits; luck does definitely not come into it.

A question that often comes up in photographic conversation is how many pictures a photographer should shoot on an assignment to get successful results. Each individual photographer will operate in his own way, some taking more shots than others, but bear in mind, if it's a 'hot' news story you will be lucky to over-shoot. It is the weak stories that photographers are inclined to over-shoot on. If a photographer is covering a feature for a magazine and is required to photograph in black and white plus colour, it is obvious he will be taking more exposures than a photographer covering a football match. So the debate can go on, and this question never really gets answered. But I say this and believe it to be correct – a good competent photographer will take only what is photographic; he will know what is and what is not worth photographing. His photography will be that much superior. Too many photographers are over-shooting; they do not know when to take the finger off the button when using a motor-driven camera. They are just not selective or competent enough when using this type of equipment. Anyone can take hundreds of bad photographs on an assignment, but on the other hand it is really hard to take hundreds of good ones.

While working on good picture taking be careful not to become too contrived or corny. Set-up pictures are acceptable with a human interest situation, but not on a news story or a serious feature story. What is contrived and what is not is a very debatable subject. A photograph that is blatantly faked, posed, created only in the imagination of the photographer's mind and misrepresenting the mood of events – this to me is contrived. Good human interest pictures of children and animals taken by photographers with a sense of humour are very acceptable; they bring a little happiness to our lives each day. A sports photographer might create a set-up photograph for effect by placing cameras in difficult positions to give another dimension to his photography. I once clamped a camera to my boots while doing a parachute jump and this produced a very effective photograph (see photo 4). This is not contrived photography.

It is the photographer with ability who can translate a paragraph of a few words into a photograph that sums it all up. He is an asset to a newspaper. One of these, for example, is Alistair Macdonald of the *Daily Mirror*. He has produced several memorable photographs, and one I can remember was taken of a house near London Airport that was right under the flight-path of the planes that take off and land there. A photograph of the house with one plane flying over the top would not be all that interesting, but Alistair made a multi-exposure plus composite photograph which showed many aircraft in the sky, giving a feeling of what it was like to live in that house. The *Daily Mirror* published it large-size and gave it the space it really deserved.

The idea I had for one of my own set-up pictures (photo 1) came after reading a small news paragraph saying that the one hundred and ninety-eighth soldier had been shot dead in Northern Ireland. It made me angry that so little space had been given to such an important item. I felt that Northern Ireland was being taken for granted; to me it was important – I had worked in Ireland many times, covering the situation. Knowing that within a short time the two-

hundredth British soldier would be killed, I made two hundred wooden crosses at home in my garden, and planted them in a field in the Surrey countryside on the day after the two-hundredth British soldier was killed. The *Daily Express* used it – a full half-page – and it brought home to the reader the tragic loss of life. I would like to add that the social commentary type of photograph should not be taken for financial gain. The photographer at times must allow himself to become involved in issues he feels strongly about; covering one's cost is different to making a profit. A photographer must give something back to photography. It is these pictures that can bring home the importance of life. The photograph was eloquent, and the event did not just end up tucked away as a small paragraph saying merely 'Another British soldier was shot dead in Belfast'.

A good photographer must always be aware of what is happening around him at all times, even when he is working on an assignment; he must watch other events. His mind must take in all possibilities of producing good photographs. There are some photographers who excel at visualising good picture ideas; others' personality and perseverance gets them into situations that give them scoops, even though their technical ability may not be as good as others'. So many ingredients go into the making of a good photographer. Keenness is one of the essentials. I think most photographers at the beginning have keenness, but it needs real interest and dedication to maintain it through the years. It is this keenness that keeps a photographer working doggedly on an assignment until he has made his pictures, a keenness that will keep him on edge until he knows his pictures have been developed and have come out as he expected. There is a great feeling of exhilaration when one has got a really great photograph, and the experience of seeing your byline under its publication in a newspaper that will be seen by millions is equally rewarding.

When you first start out in photo-journalism you're striving your hardest to produce good pictures from your assignments; you will feel nervous, but not in the way you would on the assignments I referred to earlier – ones that are hair-raising and start the adrenalin going through your body. I know photographers of many years' experience who suffer from nervous tension. Even today, when covering the most mundane story, I sometimes find myself feeling edgy and a little apprehensive about what I can produce on the subject at hand. Still, in some ways this is a good sign for you are not taking anything for granted;

being concerned will make you think that much more positively, for it is dangerous to underestimate any assignment. On the other hand, to make the most out of a difficult subject you must be completely confident in your photographic ability, and able to use all your photographic knowledge to produce the desired effect. Obviously, the more practical use you make of applying your technique the more proficient you become, but be content at first to perfect your photography stage by stage. Presumably, if you are employed on a newspaper or magazine, you will have a good knowledge of photography, if only in black and white.

If you have decided that the life of a free-lance photo-journalist is what your future is to be, then of course a good sound knowledge of colour is something you must have, for you will certainly be required to do both monochrome and colour on many of your assignments. Another thing you must learn in good picture taking is how to communicate with your subjects. By this I mean when photographing people rich or poor, famous or not so famous; for many of them it will be the first time in their lives they have had any dealings with a newspaper man, and they may never do so again. The story that has brought them into the news is probably already an unnerving experience for them. Put them at their ease. A photographer must have good manners and show an understanding of the way they feel. Even with the famous the Press at times take them for granted, but they can be on edge and also very shy. It is a good photographer who is aware of the mood and feelings of his subject who achieves the best photographs. Some say that having a thick skin in photo-journalism is an advantage; maybe so, but how thick a skin I would not like to hazard a guess. I think determination, with a certain amount of nerve, is a far better combination. Call it cheek if you like, with a polite, persuasive manner added. If there is time I try and explain to my subject what I am trying to achieve. If they disagree they can only say 'No'; more often than not it is 'Yes'.

Having said earlier that luck plays a part in taking good news pictures, and that technique and ability is needed for other kinds of photographic jobs, I would like to give another practical and personal experience of using technique. Years ago, while working with a large format camera and an electronic flash (which was then in its infant days, very bulky and heavy), I would often use the flash on bright sunny days as a 'fill-in', at the same time using a three-times yellow filter on my lens to bring out dark skies and give good cloud effects. It gave a very pleasing effect, and often my photographs were published in preference to pictures from the other agencies.

Since those early experiences with daylight flash, I have now put it into much more effective use with a 35mm camera. For instance, one story I had to cover was of a young couple hit by a tragic illness. Now photographing people who are unwell is in itself difficult, but another factor that I had to contend with was that they were not photogenic. It is an inescapable fact that we are not all creatures of great beauty – on the contrary – and a photographer must find beauty in character, light or in whatever form it may be. Beauty is indeed in the eye of the beholder. In our case, being photographers, we must capture it, and capture it with the camera. This particular story of two young courageous people brought close together by illness was more straightforward for the reporter – the story was heart-rending. For me, it was difficult. How could I do justice to the story and get my pictures into the paper with the space the story deserved? If I photographed them close up it would probably have only made two columns or even less.

On our drive from London to the home of the couple I had remarked to the reporter on the beauty of the cloud formation, and this gave me the idea for my photograph. Leaving the reporter to interview the couple, I went in search of a possible location nearby. I found an old gate behind which was a backcloth of clouds, back-lit by the sun. I returned to the couple and my colleague and told them my idea of the photograph. Fortunately, the reporter was an understanding and very professional journalist who realised that the better the photograph, the more space he would have in the newspaper. I got the young couple to pose, leaning on the gate with the sky as the background, and this is where technique came in – I wanted to get maximum cloud effects but not to lose the subject in silhouette. Recalling the experience of my early days, but now working with my 35mm camera fitted with a 21mm wide-angle lens, I used a fill-in flash at a distance of 15 feet, held by the reporter high above his head to avoid over-flashing. The film I was using was a black and white 400 A.S.A. with a three-times yellow filter for maximum cloud effects and an aperture of f16 with a speed of 1/60th of a second. I positioned myself at about ten feet from the subject and the effect I was after was perfect.

Next day the picture was used as photo-news in the *Daily Express*. Not standing too close to the couple and using the wide-angled lens helped not to overemphasise their not being photogenic. Clouds gave a romantic, yet sad, effect that was in keeping with the story. I would like to give credit to the darkroom printer who was an important contributor to the final result, for he understood what I was trying to achieve with the clouds and subject.

This is one of many techniques photographers learn. I have used it on numerous other occasions and still do today, for photographing unphotogenic people and film stars alike, and I once used it on a news story at the time of the abolition of capital punishment, the subject being former hangman Albert Pierrepoint who had executed over 400 people. Pierrepoint himself disagreed with capital punishment and supported its abolition. I needed a dramatic picture to sum up the events that were happening at this time. Albert had agreed to come with me to a certain spot to pose for my photograph. Here again I used the sky technique, with a flash some distance off mounted on a tripod, shooting into the light and with a three-times yellow filter. I also framed in my photograph a tree without leaves which looked like the old-fashioned hangman's tree, to give it more effect. This photograph was spread right across the centre-spread of the *Sun* and was used many times to illustrate items about hanging. I was satisfied with the result of the photograph; it was strong and had impact and to me it was good photography. This is what good picture taking is all about – having created something you are satisfied with yourself, that will please and interest others and will also be of use editorially.

Something I always try to remember – one successful assignment leads to another. There is a snowball effect. People become aware of your work and capabilities, and success in itself aids you in your photography.

1. Lest We Forget

Two hundred crosses planted in a Surrey field. My aim was to show the utter waste of life in this troubled area. Each cross represented a British soldier killed in Northern Ireland. Although the photograph was used and helped to get the message home, I now see that the crosses are lost in the overall scene and should have been much larger. It took three days to set this picture up, making the crosses and planting them in suitable location, time I feel well spent.

I used a 35mm camera with 35mm lens, the speed 1/60 second at f16 on Tri X film.

2. Portrait of Enoch Powell

It was after some considerable effort and letter writing that I managed to get a photographic session with Mr Powell. He told me that it was due only to my perseverance that permission was eventually granted. I took this close-up (full frame) exactly as printed; I found his face had a fascinating character, something brought on just that much more by a close-up picture.

The lighting was bounced flash, straight into a single white umbrella about two yards from the subject, the same distance as the camera. Shot with a 85mm lens on a 35mm camera with an aperture of f8, the film Kodak Tri X.

3. Lord George Brown

I changed my usual lighting set-up on this shot of Lord George Brown because I wanted to avoid reflection in his glasses; the strong side and back-lighting came through the white mesh curtains, and I used bounced flash from the ceiling to help fill in shadows between his glasses and face.

The 35mm camera was fitted with an 85mm lens, aperture was f8 at 1/60 second on Tri X film.

4. Anything for a picture

I took this photograph of myself during a parachute jump while training with the Paras. I fixed a 35mm camera with a fisheye lens to the top of my boot, using a motor drive with release cable fixed under my clothes – and then just simply fired away once I'd left the balloon.

The exposure was 1/500 second at f8 on Tri X film.

5. Glamorous Legs Contest

A colleague of mine gave me the tip about his 90-year-old uncle who was judging a glamorous legs contest. This is the type of event that happens around us daily and makes good feature material.

I used a 35mm lens with an aperture of f11 and a flash to clean up the shadows; the shutter speed was 1/60 second.

6. & 7. Graveyard for Warplanes

These photographs happened by chance, or rather, by keeping my eyes open, stumbling on a story from which quite a lot of money was made in syndication rights. While driving between Tucson, Arizona, to Tombstone I noticed in the distance hundreds of tails glinting in the sun. Making a detour I came across a giant United States Airforce base which is the graveyard for most of their old planes. stored in the desert because of the dry climate. They were valued at over six billion dollars. The aeroplanes include B52 bombers (used to bomb Vietnam), hundreds of helicopters and jet fighters and an old Presidential 707 Boeing.

However, nobody can just walk in and start taking photographs of any military establishment, so I carried on to Tombstone to cover my other story and from there spent two days setting up the necessary permission to photograph these aircraft.

The photographs were taken from the top of a very tall cherry picker (a turntable crane used for maintenance of the aircraft); both were taken on a 28mm lens with a three-times yellow filter at a speed of 1/60 second at f16. The pictures look straightforward but it took over five hours to get them set up. It was difficult placing the cherry picker in the right position to get the angles I needed; I wanted sufficient elevation to show the vast number of aircraft running right into the background, but getting height emptied the foreground and had the effect of spreading the aircraft out and showing too much empty space in the foreground. A long lens did nothing to help the overall scene but was very effective for a photograph I took of a line-up of jet fighters, giving a foreshortening effect and putting them on top of each other.

18

8. Mother & Son

This type of animal picture is always in demand and usually makes money for the freelance photographer. For newspapers it is light relief, interesting to young and old alike. Most people like a pretty picture.

This shot of a Palomino and foal was taken on a 120 Rolleiflex camera with a shutter speed of 1/250 second at an aperture of f5.6, using a bounced flash set at full power to give a natural light effect. I used the larger format camera in preference to the 35mm because I was in a confined space; had I used a 35mm camera to get as much on the negative as could be achieved with the Rolleiflex, I would have needed a 35mm lens. Although this would have given me an overall sharpness I wanted to pull the subject away from the background, and the Rolleiflex with its

normal lens did just this. Using an aperture of f5.6 I did not have too much depth of focus, which helped to keep the subject clear of the background, the point of sharpness being on the heads of the animals. The bounced flash, in addition to giving a natural light effect, in fact helped to pacify the animals; a stronger direct flash would probably have upset them.

9. Ostrich

I was photographing a completely different story at the Windsor Safari Park when this fellow popped his head over the fence. It made a natural picture, with back-lighting silhouetting the hair on his neck. The 85mm lens fitted on the camera at the time was ideal – the shutter speed was 1/250 second at f8. This picture published far more than the original story I was photographing!

8

3 Ideas

The hardest part of photo-journalism is finding the idea. Events that produce pictures in themselves do not happen every day of the week. Ideas are something that a photographer must come up with time and again, whether he is staff or free-lance.

The staff photographer, even though fed with assignments by the picture desk, should throw in ideas that he thinks worth photographing. The free-lance is in a much more committed position financially – he must rely on his ability to generate picture ideas and plan ahead. He must never sit at home waiting for the telephone to ring with someone offering work, no matter how good a photographer he is.

Go out and put your ideas into practice, providing they are constructive and practicable. I know how difficult the financial side of free-lancing can be, especially for those whose story ideas may be in far-off places which are expensive to cover. Time and again photographers have approached me saying they have this idea for a tremendous story, the only trouble being that it is in some remote part of the world. When I ask if they have priced out the expenses and how much money they have, and so on, they look startled, for they seem to expect our agency or some newspaper or magazine to back them financially. In no way does this work; only the exceptional stories that stand up from the publisher's viewpoint would receive their financial backing, and then the photographer would have to be known for his ability and responsibility.

Even staff photographers have to have a very strong case in arguing that their story idea is good. The picture editor will have to put it up to the editor, who will want to know the approximate costing, as foreign assignments are very expensive and some run into thousands of pounds. They will take into account what picture value and space they can expect for the investment; would it be material that they are looking for and suitable for their magazine or newspaper, and how long would the photographer take to cover

it? Costs go up daily. It might all sound very disheartening but then, again, that is what photo-journalism is all about.

It's hard to come up with a great idea, but very easy to knock it and put it down. If you have not the financial resources to cover something you really believe in, it is very depressing, but there's always tomorrow. You get ideas from Radio and Television, talking to people and reading newspapers. It is from newspapers that I get the vast majority of my ideas. Having found an idea I check it out, making sure the story stands up, by phoning or writing; if it's an old story, can it possibly still be of interest? It seems very strange to me, but most things have been photographed before, but with a new approach you can make it look different. The free-lance stories that are not too far in travelling distance from home are the most profitable, especially the ones on your own doorstep, but to get these you must talk, look and listen to find them. Yes, they really are there and it has happened to me quite often.

On one occasion my local coalman, Jack Worsfold, called at the house. We exchanged local gossip, one thing leading to another. I discovered he was with a very famous R.A.F. squadron in the last war. As he went on I got very interested. He was a rear gunner and was shot down in a raid over France, and what's more he fell over 7000 feet without a parachute. He was stuck in the rear gun turret after the plane blew up, killing the whole of the crew except himself. Even though the event happened years ago in the war I found it fascinating and I knew others would do so. It was pointless taking dozens of pictures for I knew it would be a 'one impact shot' type story. Jack had a great face, rather mischievous and rugged, yet good-looking, especially when covered in coal-dust. I took a portrait of him in his coalyard with a sack of coal over his shoulder (photo 17).

That in itself sounds rather dull and unexciting, but knowing he had this character I was convinced that it would produce the effect and impact I was after. Using a 35mm camera fitted with a 105mm lens I took no more than 15 exposures on a Tri X film. The secret of this picture was lighting. I used a large white reflector board about two yards from the subject, shooting against the light to get back lighting. I was at about five yards from the subject. The camera speed was fast, as I did not want to use too much aperture to give me too much depth of focus – I was only after sharpness around the face. The speed was 1/500th of a second with an aperture of f8; developed in D76 I got a very good quality picture. It was used in the *Sunday Times* and published in weekly magazines, besides overseas publications.

This was a case of literally finding a story on my own doorstep, but it did not end there. A few months later the story came up again when I took Jack back to France to meet local farmers and war-time resistance fighters who helped him escape after his fall to earth. Little did I know at the time of that chance doorstep chat it would lead to this, requiring many more pictures and words and an eventual spread in the *Daily Express*, and once again it was published worldwide.

I use this particular story as an example regarding ideas. Without dwelling too much on the subject I would also like to use it to illustrate what photo-journalism is all about, for there was much more spade work behind the scenes that had to be done. After initially doing my first story on Jack the coal-man, I joined forces with a journalist colleague. A longer story had to be written and interviews done – one with Group Captain Cheshire V.C. who was the pathfinder on the raid. Another colleague of mine researched the German War Records and wrote to the Ministry of Defence for more details. In the end the combined feature was about 8000 words plus 25 pictures, which included copy photographs of wartime snaps. This to me is enlarging an idea and is complete photo-journalism, and there are potentially many subjects that crop up on one's doorstep. There is a difference in the way they fall into one's lap; one is the idea, the other is the obvious, and I will give some more examples.

My office and darkroom is at an old railway station only a few minutes' walk from my home, so over the years I have become friendly with most of the local people, from the postman to the publican, the police-man to the priest and the local garage proprietor. You name them, I know them all, and so I should in my profession. Many of these people have helped me in executing my ideas or have given me a germ of an idea to set me thinking for good pictures. One such

picture was on a very hot summer's day. News was very slack, headlines in the newspapers were about the hot weather and the radio kept on about record temperatures. I was sat sweating with my colleague and partner Paul Sargent in the railway station, trying to think up an idea as things were very flat for us also. What was needed was the old favourite, a good hot weather picture. The idea came after a short time. I remembered my friends the monks up at the monastery – if anybody should feel hot it must be them in their long robes; why not get a picture of them cooling off, paddling in the stream that runs nearby? I suggested it to Paul. Being the good newspaperman that he is, he was excited by the idea immediately. We phoned the monastery and my friend, Father Anthony, agreed to pose with two other monks. It made a wonderful picture, the monks paddling in the stream, barefooted, with robes held up to their knees. It was published all over the world and used big here in the *Sunday Mirror* (photo 10).

For this particular photograph I used a Rolleiflex 2¼ inch square camera. The camera was loaded with plus X film, the light not being very good made for a difficult exposure, with very contrasty sunlight and shade. I exposed at 1/60th of a second with an aperture of f5.6 and it gave me a very effective photograph. Some could criticise me for this photo-graph, saying it is too gimmicky or corny, but it was an amusing photograph that had human interest; it didn't misrepresent the heatwave, but in fact brought it home.

For another story, I would like to use one that I consider to be an example of the obvious – it just happened to drop into my lap and needed very little thought. Our local village policeman, while doing his rounds, often props his bike against the wall near the front door of our office, and occasionally we pass the time of day about village life and world events. He brought up the subject of the heatwave we were then experiencing and told me about a strange event happening in the next village. A man had reported an unusual plant that was growing in his back-garden. It was increasing in size by at least 12 inches a day, even though the garden was like a dust hole and had never been watered. The owner insisted he had never planted any seeds or plants. Well, the local bobby had to make another visit later that day as the Ministry of Agriculture and Fisheries had become interested and they were coming to view it. This being such an off-beat story, I went along and asked permission to take photographs. It was a limited subject for photographic scope – there is very little you can do with one rather large, tall plant! – and in my view it was not worth more than a few shots in black and white; at least, that's what I thought at the time. I used a 28mm lens on a 35mm camera. This enabled me to shoot in close and gave the effect of height to make the pictures more interesting. The *Sun* newspaper bought the story as an exclusive and used it a couple of days later. Within a short time of that publication our office was receiving enquiries from magazines and newspapers from overseas, and one from the BBC – the *Blue Peter* children's television programme – who wanted coloured stills for use that evening on their programme. Having underestimated the subject and taken no colour it meant I had to return to photograph the mystery plant once again. Luckily for me it was still growing. We processed and rushed the transparencies to London and *Blue Peter* showed several stills that evening. This is a story that is in the same category as the news story; it is not an idea conceived in the mind, it was a picture that was there for the taking.

One last example of the difference between an idea and the obvious, which helps to make my point and is a combination of the two. One evening while having a drink with my colleague Paul Sargent (yes, over a quiet drink many a good idea is thought up), Paul brought up the subject of the tiny Gurkha soldiers who would shortly be going on guard outside Buckingham Palace, relieving the traditional guardsmen. Now these small Gurkhas were being issued with large British Army overcoats for their winter-time tour of duty. None of these overcoats fitted the tiny soldiers and they were having to be tailored for each individual, and Paul thought, quite rightly too, that this would make a good photograph. We sat and discussed this at some length and threw in different permutations on how I should photograph it; in the end I came up with the idea of getting six of the shortest Gurkha soldiers wearing their little pill-box hats and six of our largest guardsmen with their tall bearskins posing for a straight-on group photograph. Paul contacted Army public relations who gave us permission for this facility exclusive to us.

Unfortunately, the day before the appointment I was sent to Northern Ireland as trouble had broken out there once again. Luckily for us Paul was able to contact Dick Swayne, one of this country's top advertising and fashion photographers, and asked him if he could help us out to cover the assignment, which he readily agreed to do. I think he enjoys the odd photo-journalist job; Dick himself, being in fashion, lives on his ability and ideas to stay at the top. We suggested the photograph we would like and Dick did photograph it that way (photo 19), as well as other photographs that he wanted to take in his own style. Still, I know he would agree that the great block buster picture was that simple full-on group shot showing these tall guardsmen, their height emphasised by the bearskins they wear, and the tiny Gurkhas with their little pill-box hats. The picture was spread in the *Daily Express* and used as a double-page spread in the old *Life* magazine a few weeks before its last issue. Dick used his Hasselblad with a normal lens and shot at a speed of 1/250 and 1/125 second at f5.6 and f8. He also shot in colour on Agfa film.

Here again is an example of successful photo-journalism, combining this time the obvious and the idea, the obvious being when Paul first picked the story up – for he knew the obvious news value of it – then how we discussed it, to come up with the final idea. There are many other examples like this. Some of these I will cover later in the book, but I will let you judge for yourselves what combination was used.

10. Cooling Off

Father Anthony (on the right) cools off with two friars during a heatwave. Hot and cold weather pictures are popular with newspapers when weather conditions are extreme. The difficulty for the photographer is to illustrate these conditions with interesting pictures; obviously a news story brought on by bad weather takes care of itself. It's during a long dull period of drought that a photographer must think of subjects other than pretty girls.

Picture taken with a 2¼ square Rolleiflex using Plus X film; the exposure was 1/60 second at f5.6.

11. Nuns Fishing

A feature picture, simple yet marketable. Unusual scenes like this are used to balance a newspaper's appearance. In its appearance and contents it is a timeless photograph; little has changed since it was taken some seven years ago. It was taken on a $2\frac{1}{4}$ square Rolleiflex camera, the shutter speed being 1/125 second with an aperture of f11, on Kodak Plus X film.

12. Lester Piggott

Lester Piggott is one of the world's truly great jockeys. He has a reputation of rarely smiling and not being very outgoing. To a photographer, knowing of the idiosyncrasies of the subject he is to photograph, it can be a bit off-putting, especially if you have travelled as far as the Bahamas.

It turned out to be one of my more pleasant assignments, getting on so well as I did with Mr Piggott and his wife Susan that on my return to England I was invited to their home in Newmarket for lunch. It illustrated for me a cardinal rule for photo-journalists – never be put off by other people's impressions.

The picture was taken on a 35mm lens using a three-times yellow filter on Tri X film at a shutter speed of 1/250 second at f11.

It shows him getting fit for the flat season which was to start several weeks later. I took the photograph to incorporate the landscape and give a feeling of sunny beaches and blue seas, hoping the picture would be used extensively in winter-time Britain's Press, for with the actual subject so small it had to have space to get my idea across.

13. Champion Jockey

Pat Eddery is one of Britain's champion jockeys. Not wanting to get the run-of-the-mill photograph of a jockey with horse, I decided to visit his home to photograph him in a nearby field with his pet dogs. It's a simple but pleasing picture, using a landscape to make the picture more interesting. In years to come the background will be as photographically pleasing as the subject.

I think whether you're a professional or amateur just wanting a happy snap, you should always try and create more interesting pictures by using good backgrounds when photographing people.

The photograph was taken on a 28mm lens at 1/125 second at f11.

14. Jack Nicklaus

This portrait is one of a series of sports personalities, commissioned for a newspaper, in which I wanted to identify the sport immediately, but at the same time provide a studio-like quality in the pictures.

Trying to tie any champion down for a photo-session is very difficult; most times you have to seize what opportunity offers. I took this picture outside the back door of the Wentworth Golf Clubhouse, just after Mr Nicklaus had returned from a successful round in a very important golf tournament.

I chose the most likely spot to grab him – I had worked this out after waiting around for three days, bearing in mind all the hangers-on and well-wishers at these events. I did not want just the normal golf picture on the course, so I set up a flash bounced into an umbrella near a large ivy-covered tree that I used as a backdrop, a few yards away from the back door (after clearing away three dustbins and a lot of mess!) I shot five exposures of this picture using a 120 Rolleiflex loaded with Plus X film, working at a speed of 1/60 second at f8, the bounced flash being three yards from the subject at a height of about six feet, with the umbrella directed towards the subject. Looking at this picture now it seems impossible that more than 30 people were also present, which was all very distracting for both me and my subject.

13

15. Keeping the Count

This picture was taken at Windsor Safari Park, set up with the help of the head lion-keeper, who is in the photograph. I doubt that it would be possible to take today, for there have been recent attacks by animals on their keepers in other game parks.

It was a simple enough picture to set up, contrived if you like, but the idea was to illustrate in one photograph the number of lions under the keeper's control. Not all the lions are in this photograph; three were in fact behind me, being kept at bay by another keeper with a long pole. Getting the lions together was easy. We put several dead rabbits up in the branches of the tree, a tasty dish no lion could refuse! I shot this photograph with a 35mm lens.

I would add that at no time should anyone get out of their car or even partly open a window; these animals move extremely fast and the power of their paws is tremendous. This picture was not taken with a foolhardy approach; the keepers knew exactly what they were doing and at all times took extreme caution.

16. Easter Bonnet

There is always a ready market for animal pictures to newspapers and children's magazines; they are also of interest internationally. Take great care when posing animals with props as they can become corny. I prefer to photograph animals naturally. On this occasion it was Fred the chimp, who was the family pet of Mary Chipperfield and enjoyed as much as any child the opportunity to dress up and show off. Fred, a lovable little character, took offence at having his photograph taken and made it very difficult for me. I used this picture in connection with an Easter Bonnet feature published as a spread in a daily paper.

Photographing animals with dark fur is difficult because you always lose detail; that is why I used a flash that was reflected off a nearby white wall and it also helped to give some light under the hat. When photographing animals or children try to avoid having too many people saying 'Look this way' or 'that way'; in the end the subject gets very confused. One person under your own direction is all that is needed.

The photograph was taken on a 2¼ Rolleiflex camera, speed was 1/125 second at f8 on Tri X film.

17. Jack the Coalman

The picture story of my local coalman is typical of
the hundreds of stories that are all around us if only
we are lucky enough to find them. Jack Worsfold
was an ex-R.A.F. tail-gunner who miraculously
escaped death when he fell 7000 feet from a bomber
that blew up on a raid over wartime France. How do
you tackle pictorially a story that happened years ago?
I wanted to keep this picture simple and not overcomplicated. One impact portrait was all that I
needed – showing him in his job and the character
he is today. Because of the nature of the story, it
needed some text to support the photograph.

On this occasion I used a large white reflector board
about two yards from the subject reflecting the
back-light onto his face. The 35mm camera was fitted
with a 105mm lens at a speed of 1/500 second at f8.

18. Winter Training

Plastic snow helps the British army to create conditions they could expect for one of their forthcoming winter exercises in Norway.

This picture was taken on a sunny afternoon on the Salisbury Plain; I used a yellow filter and back-lighting to give an air of authenticity. I chose the late afternoon light for that reason.

The 35mm camera was fitted with a 28mm lens and a three-times yellow filter working with a shutter speed of 1/250 second at f11.

19. Gurkhas and Guards
Dick Swayne, one of England's top fashion and
advertising photographers, took this photograph. He
used his Hasselblad with a normal lens, and a shutter
speed of 1/125 second at f8.

20. New Recruit

The Duke of Atholl is the only person to have his own private army – apart from the Queen. Here he views a new recruit in the lobby-cum-gun room of Atholl Castle. I decided to take this picture with this background for two reasons – the natural light was effective (though very poor) and the atmosphere had a certain tradition about it. This was one of the rare occasions when I used a tripod.

The exposure was 1/8 second at an aperture of f8. The camera was a 35mm fitted with a 35mm lens. The film, Kodak Tri X.

4 Assignments

Assignments come in a contrasting variety – from one extreme to the other. The photo-journalist must be prepared at all times to move at a moment's notice to any part of the world. Passports and vaccination certificates must be all up to date, equipment in good working order, and you must be in reasonable physical condition. The exciting thing that keeps many of us in this precarious job is the unexpected, never really knowing what is round the corner. There is no other job quite like it. Once you have left the shelter of your office you are the decision maker, your own boss. I think I have had the same satisfaction from some of my assignments as the great explorers of years ago. Taking off for the unknown is and always will be exhilarating and exciting. Mind you, I'm ruthless when it comes to family life; while others may care about everyday family events, I would willingly forsake these to be on a good assignment.

Of course, I miss my family, but I am a photo-journalist, specialising in the field of world events and there is no time to vacillate when I have to be at London Airport within the hour to catch a flight to God knows where. Magazines and newspapers are not too concerned about your personal life. The individual with excuses for not wanting to go anywhere should not be in our profession. There are many of us who live at a much slower pace and do not wish to get involved in my frenetic scene. Well, they don't know what they're missing, that's all I can say.

My camera bag is always at the ready; I'm never more than a few minutes away from it. I keep it simple and uncomplicated: three Olympus camera bodies (sometimes four if I know in advance I will be on a long assignment), plus one motor wind and one motor drive with an extension lead. My lens equipment includes a 300mm f4.5, a 150–75 mm f4 Zuko zoom, an 85mm f2 and a 28mm f2 wide-angle. Also packed are 2 small flash-guns with extension

and a small magic-eye for triggering off another flash that may be used some distance from the camera. For definition I have a well-tested two-times tele-converter, which gives me that extra range used on any lens. I carry Press cards that vary from Scotland Yard to the National Union of Journalists, and many foreign accreditation cards. My passport and vaccination certificates are always in there, together with several spare passport pictures, for these are often needed for extra accreditation when overseas or for other visas. Also, of course, a leading credit card that enables me to buy airline tickets, hire cars and pay hotel bills while travelling. This avoids worrying too much about running out of funds. Included in this rather tatty bag are spare socks, and T-shirts – which come in handy in hot climates (as well as to wrap my camera and lenses in). I carry a pocket tape-recorder and tapes for interviews and stories, a large roll of adhesive tape, marking pens and some 10 x 8 inch envelopes pre-addressed to London Airport for shipping films back to England. I carry malaria and dysentery tablets, a small screw-driver and a couple of good cigars. The cigars are for the occasions when I leave London on a flight; I might feel a little nervous and apprehensive, so I enjoy smoking one of these after take-off!

The amount of my film stock will vary from time to time, but usually when travelling overseas it is around 40 rolls of black and white Tri X, 30 rolls of colour 200 A.S.A. High speed Ektachrome, 20 rolls of 64 A.S.A. colour 64 Ektachrome plus a few rolls of Tungsten High Speed. I have one medium-sized clear plastic bag – this is for all my film, both exposed and unexposed, for when travelling I empty all my cameras, and when it comes to the security search this enables me to put my camera bag straight through the X-ray machine without fear of the X-ray affecting any of my film, as I carry the bag of film in my hand. The plastic bag enables those doing the hand-search to see your film that much quicker, making it easier for all concerned. And lastly, something I'd never travel without, a small mascot made by one of my daughters, which goes everywhere with me!

So this is my standard equipment that I carry when travelling at home or overseas. I find it adequate equipment for the majority of my work and the bag fits comfortably under an aircraft seat when making long journeys. It weighs around 32 lb; the weight is not too heavy to carry over long distances and sometimes you are required to cover quite considerable distances on foot, but you'll often be able to off-load some of your film stock at your hotel room.

I never put any films or cameras into the luggage hold of an aircraft. I make sure that they stay with me at all times as personal luggage. It does at times take some polite persuasion to enable you to do this. On the odd occasions when, for security reasons (for instance when flying from London to Belfast), my hand baggage is taken away from me at the last moment, I get a little concerned; I have seen very frustrated photographers arrive at their destination and their camera that was checked in with their general luggage has not arrived. This is dangerous practice, and remember that it can be also X-rayed at airports in random X-ray security checks.

When covering war or similar assignments, I do carry combat clothing, but I make sure it looks as civilian as possible. My combat clothing includes water-bottles and other items I may need for survival, and this of course travels with my main baggage. Photographers covering wars should never carry weapons. We are of course non-combatant, there to shoot with our cameras and not with guns. There are the times when we have to cover both sides of the conflict, and if we ever did carry arms I'm sure we would not stand much chance of living a long life.

I'd like to be able to say that I have never carried a weapon when covering trouble spots or wars, but I have recently returned from an assignment in Rhodesia where, for the first time in my life, it proved necessary to carry an automatic weapon. But I have not changed my attitude regarding newspapermen carrying weapons. Modern terrorist warfare has always been cruel, but today it has moved into a different phase – kill and let there be no survivors. The unarmed stand no chance of survival.

I have no wish to kill and was disturbed at having to carry a weapon; it was the old, old instinct – if attacked by those who would take my life, I would kill to survive.

I was travelling many miles by road in remote areas to visit farmers and other Rhodesians who lived in the bush, to report and photograph the terrorist war and its effect on their lives. Ambushes are everyday occurrences and an unarmed person would be unlikely to survive if attacked; the only chance of survival is to return the fire, holding off the ambushers until (hopefully) help arrives.

War assignments are the most difficult stories to cover, not only because of the hazardous nature of the events you become involved in. Today newspapermen are unwelcome in many parts of the world where conflict is taking place, especially in Africa where, if a photographer gets loose to picture some home truths, they know his work could cause a major world outcry. When I say this I am not referring *only* to South Africa; the Communist-backed regimes and the ambitious dictatorships elsewhere are just as anxious to control what the photographer sees, and are sensitive about his unrestricted probing and shooting. A report of a massacre can easily be denied but a photograph is another thing; it takes a lot of explaining. For this reason alone, you may not even be allowed into the country and, if you are admitted, it is more than likely you will be kept in the capital, trying to get your accreditation. Other obstacles will be put in your way, and the hope is that in time you will give up and go home.

At other times, especially in wars, we get offered what we call a 'facility' with a group of genuine newspapermen, and others who can only be described as hangers-on who are seeking a taste of adventure. I've known the number of people in such a party to be over a hundred. Many of these would-be adventurers want to try their hand at being a war-correspondent. The first bang (if they get near one), and many never come back again. I resent these amateurs playing at my profession, for war is a very emotive and difficult subject. We are not going for the twisted excitement of seeing death in battle; we are going to record the mistakes of their leaders and the soldiers who have to pay for these with their lives. That is my attitude and one that helps me to see photographs in simple subjects amid the turmoil of war.

Once a bona fide photographer has got his accreditation, he must move away from the main Press group, maybe working with a very small group just for company, for war is as frightening to the photographer as it is to the soldier, and it helps if one can share fear at times. I like to work alone or with one or two colleagues, the reason being that front line soldiers are at first very suspicious of a strange cameraman, especially at the height of a battle; they feel you have no place there and resent your intrusion on their personal grief when their comrades are killed or wounded. Working alone you have a much lower profile, and by remaining with them over a long period of time you get to know them and you become part of their unit. As you carry no weapon and, unlike them, don't *have* to be there, they respect you for it, and feel protective towards you. The photographs taken in these situations could possibly be the most historic or the best you will ever take in your career, so it is absolutely essential that you make sure your photography is right. Do not click off blindly – look for the individual or incident that means something or says something about your own experience of the action.

The equipment I carry into the field is what I normally carry at home on all my assignments. I have two cameras around my neck, one fitted with a 28mm lens and the second with a 75mm to 150mm zoom or an 85 mm lens (changing to longer lenses if needed, always at hand in my bag). One camera is loaded with colour, the others with black and white. In the field I carry about 15 black and white films and 20 colour. Exposed films go into a spare plastic bag. I mark films then and there for identification purposes as I take them out of the camera, particularly if it's something that's special, or that will need adjusting in developer. Of course I keep my captions up to date and always ready to ship with the films back to the office at a moment's notice. I have mentioned that I have envelopes etc. with me – the best pictures don't mean a thing left in the camera bag. Several times I have been in some remote location when by pure chance somebody has come along who has managed to take my films for shipping. To my amazement, I have never lost one packet, but I make sure the carrier is reponsible, for shipping films can be very complicated and some people just do not have that sense of urgency.

My favourite lenses for this kind of work are the 85mm f2 or the 28mm f2. They give me the range I need, as at times I'm right on top of the incidents when one needs a wide angle to take pictures without distorting the incident. At other times the 85mm enables you to be unobtrusive in a sensitive situation. War can be uncannily silent when you have the disturbing sound of a motor-drive buzzing away. Try picking your pictures in these moments of tranquillity. War is very difficult to photograph. I've been in a battle when thousands of rounds have been fired, and I just had to keep my head down. It's impossible to photograph flying bullets! Shelling, if it's outgoing (from your side) requires luck, like a photograph I took in Vietnam of the shells leaving the muzzles of the U.S. guns. If it's incoming artillery falling

in the vicinity, I say a prayer and once again keep my head down. Pictures are more often produced after these incidents in which men were killed or wounded by fragmentation, but in these situations make sure you're compassionate in your picture-taking. Successful war photographers are not foolhardy, but despite their caution and experience many of my friends have been killed covering wars. It proves that you never know exactly what to expect in this type of work, and I admit it makes me think carefully before undertaking any of these assignments. I try and make sure I know what I'm letting myself in for.

War does strange things to photographers; most of the ones I know get emotionally involved, and this brings out the best in them photographically. At times they may give the impression of being hard and cynical or of having some political axe to grind, but whatever attitudes others see in them can be totally wrong. Yes, of course we get angry about power-grabbing politicians and other self-seekers – we see their dirty work – but the photographer is usually a very compassionate person who is deeply affected by war and other human tragedies. Death is a familiar sight to the war photographer; he passes the dead without so much as a second glance – as any combat soldier must do if he is to remain effective – but there are times when he will be fixed to the spot at the sight of a human being lying in the loneliness of death in some dusty field; all the horrors of war are suddenly brought home to him. The dead had relatives somewhere; a telegram will come and the shattering effect will change their lives forever.

Newspapers rarely publish detailed pictures of people killed in war – the agony and horror that the dead may have suffered are too real for the breakfast table – though some magazines will carry such pictures. Whether publication is a good or bad thing is for the reader to decide. My personal view is that it must be recorded and seen; otherwise the rest of the world will be oblivious to the suffering and degradation that war brings. Such horrific scenes cannot be photographed other than with compassion; to photograph the dead, young and old, without sympathy would degenerate into commercial sadism. I have taken a few photographs of such tragedies and in all honesty they stopped me in my tracks. Even today I can recall the exact moment and can still experience my thoughts and feelings. Death is the ultimate experience of war. I have chosen three incidents of this finality – ordinary men, all unknown to me, who are etched in my mind forever.

One picture that for me has this timeless quality was taken during the last fighting before the final fall of South Vietnam (No 32); I was with their army unit near the besieged city of Xuan Loc. A dead North Vietnamese officer lay on a blood-stained stretcher, his right arm raised in a pathetic gesture by rigor mortis. Nobody seemed to know what to do with this man as he lay in the hot sun in a dusty field being used by helicopters engaged in the war. At one time a small group of refugees fleeing from the fighting gathered round him. An official took some personal papers from his pocket, looked at letters and family photographs, then filled in some forms and returned the documents to his pocket. Soldiers were coming and going. A lone figure – a South Vietnamese paratroop officer (running from a helicopter) – turned in his tracks and glanced at the dead man. Later, when I was pulling out from this area, I noticed the body still lying there. That was in 1975; the war in Vietnam is over and probably his loved ones have had their tragedy cushioned by time. All that remains of that day is two photographs in my file; this one was taken on a 35mm camera with a 28mm lens at a speed of 1/250 second at f11.

Wherever a war is fought, were it Paradise itself, life soon disintegrates. Kyrenia to many holiday makers was a paradise until that hot June Saturday in 1974 when the Turkish invasion of Cyprus began. For the previous week Cyprus had been in turmoil and I had an uneasy feeling that a full-scale Turkish invasion was about to take place. On the Friday I positioned myself in Kyrenia, the island's picturesque harbour facing the Turkish mainland. The Turks invaded early next morning, the main landings taking place a few miles along the coast at Ayios Georgios, the prelude being strafing by Turkish jet fighters. I was driving along, trying to make my way to the beach-head with reporter Brian Parks of the *Daily Mail*, when I saw a friendly barman of the previous evening hurrying on foot in the same direction. He wore an ill-fitting uniform with a ridiculous steel helmet and carried an old British army .303 rifle. We gave him a lift; he was shaking and tense, just a young man serving with the reserves, who did not know what war was all about but had enough pride to fight for his cause – whatever it may be. We dropped him near Ayios Georgios. Brian and myself sought shelter from cross-fire in a nearby block of flats.

It was a month later when I saw that young man again as I was returning to Ayios Georgios with the Turks. He was still wearing that ridiculous helmet but this time lay face upwards in the sun, almost unrecognisable. He must have been killed soon after leaving us. This photograph has never been published

and the story was untold. The Cyprus troubles were too enormous and this small incident did not rate any importance. The picture was too horrific for a daily newspaper but it is a moment in time I shall never forget. The photograph (No 33) was taken on a 35mm camera with a 28mm lens with a speed of 1/250 second.

Another tragic scene stays vividly in my mind: the death of a young Israeli tank commander on the Golan heights. It was a sunny Tuesday during the Yom Kippur war, when with several other photographers I was relaxing after covering tank battles and air strikes between Israeli and Syrian forces. We were at a crossroads, trying to find a reasonably safe way to travel; suddenly a tank came rumbling with some urgency to a halt beside a field ambulance unit that was stationed nearby. Crewmen of the tank frantically beckoned the medics. Their commander had been hit in the throat by rocket fragments. They lifted him gently down in his last moments of life onto a stretcher on the side of a dusty road. They tried desperately to save him but unfortunately he became another victim of war. The photograph was published world-wide, yet only a couple of miles up the road I had seen two Syrian tank crewmen lying dead beside their tank. We were all slightly mesmer-ised by this sight as they all looked so peaceful in death, unmutilated and not at all horrific. These photographs, as far as I know, made very little space in the media, but the tragedy was the same for all families.

It was some months later I received a letter from an Israeli girl who believed the young Israeli was her boyfriend, killed on the Golan Heights. She had seen the tragic photograph and she wanted to know exactly what happened, the location and time of his death. She wrote that they had spent many happy days on the Golan Heights and had loved it, and she told me of her boyfriend's love for the Heights. A keen photographer, he had photographed the flowers and the birds. It seemed ironic that I should recall his death due to the violence of war, but unlike many others he did not die in some strange forgotten field. These photographs are also in my file.

The picture of the dead Israeli tank commander (No 34) was taken on a 135mm lens at 1/250 at f8. The dead Syrian crewman (No 35), on a 28mm lens at 1/250 at f11.

There are more pleasant assignments I cover, though not necessarily as rewarding, in terms of its meaning for life, to one's inner feelings, either emotionally or photographically. In some strange way war does satisfy; still, the enjoyable soft-feature type of assignment does need good picture-taking, and use of your ability and technique. These jobs can also give great satisfaction, especially the ones you create yourself from nothing.

One I particularly enjoyed was on the tiny island of Papa Stour, which is a small island off the main Shetland Islands. The story was about the smallest school in the world – smallest not in size but in the number of staff and pupils attending it. There were just one teacher and one little girl pupil. People had emigrated from this island over the years until only the Postmistress's family was left, as well as the school-teacher. It took me several days trying to trace the island. Then I phoned up to fix my appointments. Having done this, I flew to the Shetlands, hired a car and a boat, and arrived one morning after a night of heavy snow. The skies were now sunny and blue – a gift for picture-taking in itself – but I needed good impact in my photographs to make it stand up for the daily newspapers.

The feature-type pictures for magazines were there for the taking – the little girl amidst empty desks in the schoolroom, getting ready for the Christmas Nativity play, the teacher still carrying on the complete school curriculum – all providing good pictures in colour. I was shooting half in black and white and half in colour, and was getting enough general material, but I still did not have that one shot showing the loneliness of these two in their little school once filled with the laughter and noise of a hundred pupils. I was getting a little frustrated at being able to take so many good pictures and yet still not coming up with one I needed to do justice to the story. I decided to walk round the outside of the school careful not to make too many footprints in the snow. It looked such a picturesque setting.

Then the idea came – a school group with the school as the background. I sat a bench in the snow, again careful only to make one set of footprints, then sat teacher and pupil in the dead centre for the annual school group; it gave me that strong main photograph (No 39). I used a three-times yellow filter to give me contrast in the sky, snow and shadow. Working on Tri X film, the aperture was f16 at a speed of 1/125 second. I got exactly the picture I was after for my main splash. I'm always careful to get full exposure negatives in bright light, especially when working in snow or the desert, where you find the extreme shadows due to sunny conditions. To me there is nothing worse than no exposure in the shadows where it's gone 'glassy', losing all detail. The ink of newspapers printing in black and white can lose it even more. In colour it is not quite so difficult, for something seems to get held there, so it does look effective when you're shooting this way.

As the teacher and the little girl got up and walked away another evocative picture was produced. They walked hand-in-hand straight towards the sun, casting a long shadow behind. I quickly stepped up my speed to 1/500 second. I wanted a silhouette effect; still with an aperture of f16 and using the yellow filter, I took my final photograph of the session which gave me an end to my story (No 40). On this Shetland assignment I was using exactly the same type of equipment that I used a few months before in Vietnam.

21–31. Vietnam

Vietnam produced many remarkable photographers.
No war has ever been photographed so thoroughly
and in such depth; thousands of pictures were taken
by experienced and inexperienced photographers who
flocked there in their hundreds during the years the war
was fought. Many award-winning pictures were taken,
yet the vast majority of the photographers' work is
still unpublished today, due to the fact that immediate
news pictures with impact were daily available to
the world's press. There were many that showed the
magnitude of this conflict, taken by the very experienced
photographers who combined action and feature
pictures which filled the pages of weekly magazines.
But it is the thousands of unused exposures that
interest me: the picture that looked interesting at the
time that you *had* to take, for these too tell a story. If
you look only as far as death or a blood-stained
bandage for your interpretation of war you would
indeed be a very shallow photographer.

Vietnam was an event which saw the coming of age
of the dedicated photo-journalist in the true sense.
It also saw the coming of age of the 35mm camera as
we know it today. It was not until the late Fifties and
early Sixties that it finally became the most used
camera for our work internationally, in both war and
sports photography. Of course, it was used by many
great photographers before this period, but it was at
this time that the darkrooms and photographers in
most newspapers got to grips with processing and
using miniature film. Before this, there was appre-
hension about using the 35mm due to the inferior
quality they produced compared with a large format.
The manufacturer of better quality film combined
with the development of more sophisticated cameras
proved a God-send to the photographers who were
expected to keep up with the jet age and instant
communications. In Vietnam, photographers used
their cameras to the limit – in all conditions it was a
proving ground for reliability.

The helicopter played an important part in Vietnam,
and it also proved a blessing to the photo-journalist.
The photographer with his compact equipment could
move easily and be rapidly transported from one battle
zone to another. This airborne facility was there for
all the accredited war correspondents, enabling us to
cover the area of our choice. I don't believe these
facilities will be quite so freely offered in any future
war. The photographers and television newsmen in
Vietnam exposed war, with all its violence, to practi-
cally every home in the world. Whether that was
right or wrong I don't know, but it did cause political
embarrassment and greatly weakened morale in
America and among its soldiers in the field. In all
honesty it may have undermined security; photographers from all over the world could operate freely
with the American press but there was little if any
facility offered by North Vietnam. Future conflicts

are only going to be hard for the photo-journalist to cover; probably only a few official photographers will actually cover the fighting, their material being censored by the military, but whatever war we get involved in we must, as I have said, look further than a blood-stained bandage.

I have selected a few from my Vietnam picture coverage; the day-to-day type of photograph one would be expected to get on such assignments. All but two of these were taken shortly before the eventual fall of the South to Northern armies.

The first two pictures were taken on previous visits there. No 21 shows a wounded U.S. soldier the morning after a night of shelling on a hill near Kha Shan. This is the sort of picture one would be taking while operating with forward troops – not sensational, but portraying an inevitable incident. I feel the picture is of more significance today than when taken.

The same applies to picture No 22; this shot was taken while I was working with an Australian unit and it shows a VC (Viet Cong) being taken prisoner. This picture could without proper captioning easily be misunderstood, for at first glance it looks as if the prisoner is being manhandled; in fact the poor chap was terrified of the helicopter he was being taken to, and the blast of the swirling blades helped to give this very ordinary picture more movement. Both pictures were taken on a 35mm camera fitted with 35mm lens.

No 23 was taken in Saigon a few days before the fall of the capital. It shows the last Cub Scouts' meeting taking place in the gardens in front of the Presidential palace. It seems incredible to me that the young Cub-mistress could carry on so normally, for in the distance gunfire could be heard as the final battles were fought outside the city. Looking at this picture today I wonder what became of these young Cubs. The photograph was taken on 35mm camera with 35mm lens.

Nos 24–30 are taken in and around the besieged town of Xuan Loc just before it fell to the Communist forces. Picture No 24 shows blindfolded captured North Vietnamese soldiers. No 25 shows wounded South Vietnamese soldiers waiting to be flown out by helicopter from the surrounded town. No 26 shows a helicopter rescuing wounded South Vietnamese from the town of Xuan Loc. All these pictures were taken on a 35mm camera using a 35mm lens. No 27 shows a helicopter coming in to re-supply and rescue wounded. This picture was taken on a 105mm lens as were Nos 28, 29 and 30.

Picture No 28 shows a wounded woman being evacuated from Xuan Loc, No 29 is of exhausted children resting after being rescued from the town, and then No 30 – with an air of dejection a man and his family shelter from the intense heat under an umbrella – one of his few remaining possessions.

No 31 – I was sheltering with these American soldiers from North Vietnamese shelling during the fighting to relieve the besieged American Marine base at Kha Shan. With me was my good friend and colleague Larry Burrows, the *Life* photographer, who was later killed there. This is one of these occasions which one remembers as if it only happened yesterday. It was on Hill Timothy, to which Larry and I had flown on the first stage of this gigantic helicopter operation; we were stuck there for two nights.

The first night we dug a small hole just big enough for us to get into, intending it to give us shelter from the damp mist that comes down at night, but it sheltered us from more than that during the night, as we had very heavy incoming shelling killing and injuring American soldiers near us.

The picture was taken on a 35mm lens, at 1/125 second at f5.6.

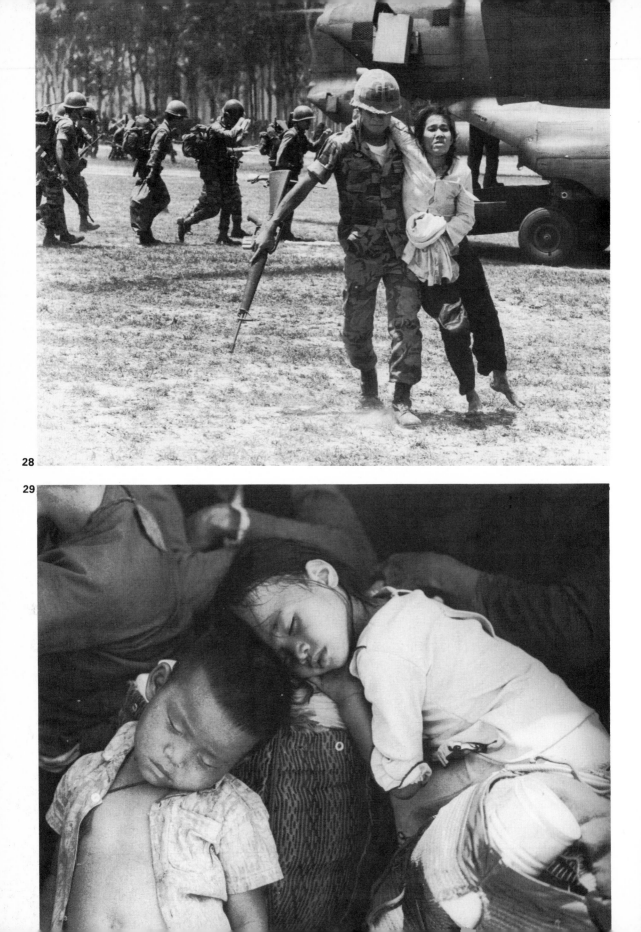

36

37

38

36–38. Israeli War

Three more pictures from the Yom Kippur war.

No 36 (Above left) shows Israeli tanks going into action on the Golan Heights. This picture was taken on a 135mm lens and with the same lens I photographed a member of an Israeli tank crew praying before going into action, also on the Golan Heights (No 37) (Left).

The picture of these Egyptian prisoners (No 38) was taken after the Israelis had crossed the Suez Canal. The prisoners were waiting to be shipped back to prisoner of war camps. It was taken on a 28mm lens.

39 & 40.   Smallest School in the World

Two pictures from a series showing school life on the
tiny remote island of Papa Stour in the Shetlands.
The lighting condition caused me problems similar
to those I would have expected in tropical Africa –
bright sun with dark heavy shadows. I'm always very
careful not to over-expose in these circumstances;
if you do the shadow detail goes completely. Photographing on this assignment for both newspapers
and magazines, I knew that these particular two
pictures were all that a daily newspaper would require,
and would sum up the story simply and quickly with
a caption of not more than 200 words. The group
picture was published as a half page.

    For both of these pictures I used a 28mm lens with
a three-times yellow filter – the group was taken at
1/125 second at f16. The silhouette was 1/500 second
at f16. The camera was loaded with Tri X.

41. Wild Geese

This is a scene from the film 'Wild Geese', starring Richard Burton, Roger Moore and Richard Harris. This part of the film was shot near the Rhodesian border with South Africa. I took this picture on high-speed Ektachrome 160 A.S.A. film from which a black and white negative was made.

I try to avoid doing this usually, for you do lose a certain quality in the black and white print, but at times there is no alternative. Here, for instance, was a potentially dangerous stunt for the pilot. The scene was set up by the special effects people and was ready to go after a couple of rehearsals – then the real thing. They blew up the bridge and lorries to make it look as if the dummy bomb dropped by the plane as it raced overhead was real. Timing had to be perfect. With a moving film it was comparatively easy – there was a continuous sequence – but the still picture would be useless if shot too early or too late. Too early, and the plane would be too small and the explosion would not be reaching its maximum height, a fraction later, and the plane would have been out of the picture frame.

I could not guarantee that my camera fitted with a motor drive would synchronise with the action, so I decided to use 'single frame' and wait until the aircraft was almost out of the finder. In fact, this was the best and most impressive shot. I did expose two frames quickly before this but the aircraft appeared too small.

For these photographs I used an 85mm lens working at a 1/500 second at f11.

42. Tombstone, Arizona, 1976

This picture of the city marshal of Tombstone was taken by very early-morning light, giving the effect I felt suited a bygone age. Each day while in Tombstone on this assignment I started work at dawn, for I knew that the light was all that had not changed over the past 100 years, that it was the only real thing left for me to photograph and would give me a true dramatic effect of the days when Virgil Earp was city marshal.

A photographer who never bothers to discover the light of a 24-hour period must miss so many pictures. The atmosphere of any city, town or village is so different at mid-day from the still hour of first light – or dusk as the town people go scurrying home.

The picture was taken on a 35mm camera with a 28mm lens, the speed 1/60 second at f11.

5 Royal Photographers

A member of the British Royal family attracts more publicity and coverage than any other single person or story.

Man's landing on the moon produced historic and famous pictures; at the time it filled our newspapers and magazines, but today it is past history. The Queen, when Princess Elizabeth, had the same space on her wedding day, and again when her father died and she became Queen while on a visit to Africa. Historic pictures took up many column inches of the Coronation in newspapers and magazines throughout the world, and of course Royal tours and other events involving Her Majesty and other members of the Royal family have been similarly treated.

Hardly a day goes by when one Royal story or another is not used in some part of the world. For this reason I feel no book covering photographic journalism would be complete without a Royal section.

At times reporters have to write their stories on hearsay or chit-chat, for the Royal family rarely gives exclusive interviews. It's on Royal tours that reporters can get more intimate and accurate reporting. Photographers do have more opportunities on unofficial engagements for the good still picture that shows them at work and play but, like reporters, very few Fleet Street photographers get special facilities to photograph the Royal family, except on official occasions, which usually results in a very staid type of photograph.

It is the demand for the more informal and everyday picture that has helped create a group of 'Royal' photographers, not officially recognised and yet not unknown to Buckingham Palace. I would make it clear that these photographers are not Paparazzi – they abide by and respect the wishes of the Royal family.

Their conduct at times may be a little over-enthusiastic behind the scenes but is, I believe, acceptable to the Royal family, for these photographers do a wonderful job in humanising them. Their photographs are not distasteful or discourteous; most are taken with the Royal family's tacit consent showing them enjoying a normal life.

A photographer covering Royal events must endure long hours and many frustrations, finding it difficult to produce good, interesting material all the time, as most official engagements have a sameness about them. Often photographers are placed in the worst possible position by inexperienced officials (not connected with Buckingham Palace), who don't realise Royal tours are there to promote goodwill and need a good Press coverage to do just that.

There is a code of conduct that photographers must observe when covering Royal occasions and other assignments where protocol is required; for instance, dress is important – when to be informal or formal. At times this is not easy with cameras hanging around one's neck, especially in very hot climates, but we should always try to dress appropriately, no matter what the occasion.

Recently I witnessed a none-too-pleasant scene at the third wedding of King Hussein of Jordan. There was a gathering of eighty international photographers for the occasion in Amman, all of whom were invited to the Royal Palace for the wedding reception which took place in the Palace grounds, amongst beautifully laid-out flower beds and special floral arrangements. As with all these events, a number of photographers who seem very unprofessional turned up. We had all been asked to wear suits and ties, but one turned up in a white T-shirt with a slogan emblazoned across his chest. Ladies in elegant dresses were pushed aside by photographers trying to get in front of the King and his bride; flowers were trampled on and the floral displays upset, and at one point the tall wedding cake looked as though it might be toppled over.

Fortunately in England we usually avoid these scenes, for selected organisations put in a 'pool' photographer, although at times I feel the method of allocation is a little unfair.

Television gets far better facilities than the still photographer, even though they may require a three- or four-man crew and they and their equipment are much more obtrusive. Television is also given the opportunity of making in-depth TV films of the Royal family and other interesting people, which probably take months to make and a lot of personal time on the part of those whom they are portraying. A stills photographer afforded an official session would be expected to complete in minutes rather than hours. This is why there is a need for the unofficial Royal photographers who produce good informal pictures of our Royal family, and credit must be given to them for dedication and patience in producing these. The majority are free-lancers and most, I hope, make a reasonable living doing it, for it certainly would take a very complex and experienced public relations organisation to do the job as well.

43–52. Royal Photographers

43. Prince Charles dancing the Samba in Rio during a Royal tour of Brazil. The 35mm camera was fitted with a 28mm lens with a shutter speed of 1/60 second. The flash was set on automatic to give an f8 setting and exposures in quick succession, with my motor drive set on single frames. I used one of the small popular electronic flashes on both my cameras, one loaded with colour. The aperture (for Ektachrome 200 A.S.A.) was f5.6. On these occasions it's lucky that any photograph ever comes out, for at times you are shooting completely blind; there are photographers jostling each other, the crowds pushing the photographers and the police pushing the crowds, not to mention a near-nude lady with lots of feathers who wanted to samba and grabbed me while I was trying to take this picture!

44. A picture that nearly made it, but not quite. It is just a little too official. It shows the Queen talking to local Indians during her 1978 tour of Canada. The lens was a 28mm with a shutter speed of 1/250 second at f11.

45. This picture of Prince Edward was taken in a mine half a mile underground during the Royal Tour of Canada. The 85mm lens was an ideal combination with the flash, and was helped by television lights giving some back-lighting. The aperture was f8 at 1/60 second.

46. For this close-up of the Queen I used my 300mm lens. It shows her enjoying a rodeo during her Canadian tour. The shutter speed was 1/125 second at f8.

47. Princess Anne weighs-in for a riding event. The picture was taken in poor light on an 85mm lens; the aperture was f4 at a speed of 1/125 second.

48. There is always the incident the photographer must look for on Royal tours – such as this unrehearsed incident during the Queen's tour of Canada. It was taken on the 75mm–150mm zoom.

49 & 50. These pictures were taken of Prince Charles during his visit to Ghana. Both were taken with a 300mm lens, which illustrates the value of the telephoto lens on official engagements. The exposure was the same in both shots, 1/125 second at f5.6.

51. Prince Andrew is always popular with the ladies. The picture is taken on the 300mm lens at a shutter speed of 1/250 second, at f8.

52. Prince Charles visits a tribal chief during his tour to Ghana, wearing fitting dress for the occasion. A small flash gave an aperture of f8 on 28mm lens.

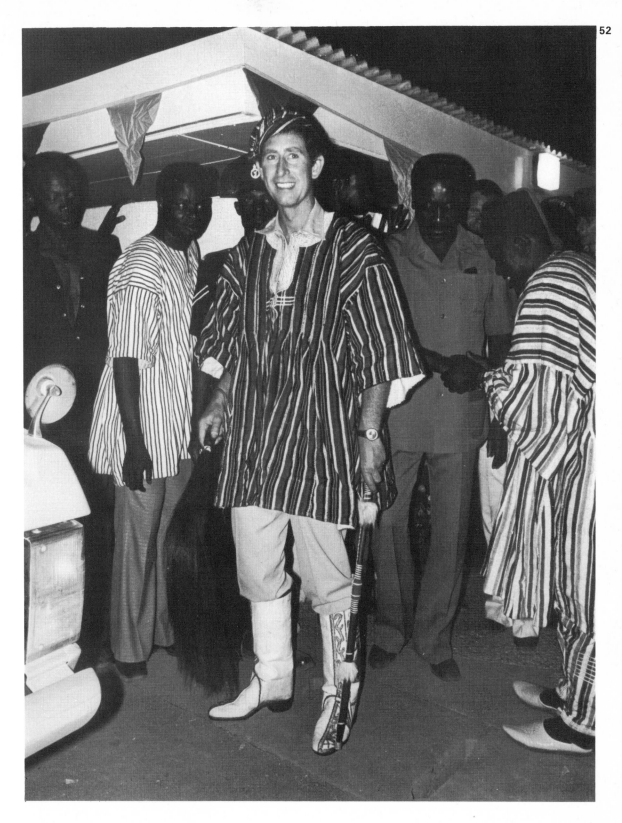

6 Glamour and Fashion

Glamour photography today is certainly playing an important part in the circulation of certain daily newspapers. Just a few years ago a naked breast would have caught your eye only in the glamour magazines, but today it is a regular feature of our popular dailies. The 'page three' girls are something that is here to stay. I think the majority are presented with reasonably good taste, as harmless entertainment – for that's what it is. Being a photo-journalist, I sometimes wonder whether glamour photography really is photo-journalism; then again, in the course of my work I do take on a glamour assignment, but at the same time I try not to lose my identity and become just a glamour photographer. Mind you, the photographers who specialise in glamour are some of the best I know, turning out superb quality pictures that I envy. In this field quality is something that is a must, for anything less looks tatty. The models themselves also have to be good – elegant and well-groomed. Another reason why glamour and fashion must be included with photo-journalism is that it takes up so much newspaper space, not only in England but all around the world. Glamour and show business together probably takes up over a third of a newspaper.

Glamour photography exacts the best in a photographer, requiring the maximum in technical ability. Creating something beautiful is a challenge to anyone, for this creativity is what is required by the picture editors who need glamour material.

The fashion photographers who specialise in taking pictures for the fashion pages of newspapers or magazines are of a similar type. Their requirements are the same: creativity and technical quality – except that clothes replace the flesh – and an understanding of what and how fashion can be photographed. They each have their own techniques, whether on location or in the studio. They have the same problems in the studio: they can only permutate the strobe lighting in a limited number of ways, and so similarities must appear in some of the pictures. On location there is more opportunity to be different in the way photographers use back-lighting, their ability to see tiny things such as a good background, the gnarled wood of an old door, or attractive brickwork that may be covered in ivy. They can decide how best to use a long lens to combine subject and background together, the subject pin-sharp and background out of focus. Many photographers doing this type of work either use a 105mm or a 135mm lens with a 35mm camera, working with a rather wide aperture so as to give them that fuzzy background. To achieve still better quality they work with slower films, or larger format cameras such as the Hasselblad. I find an ideal lens for this format is a 150mm lens which still works on the same principle – subject sharp and background muzzy.

I must say that the glamour and fashion assignments that I've undertaken have proved to be exciting and rewarding photographically. I believe I must have achieved the ultimate in glamour photography when I accompanied the very glamorous and beautiful actress Julie Ege to an uninhabited desert island in the Bahamas, where we lived for a week with no food or water except for the odd fish or palm heart. It was a story of survival and glamour. My idea was to produce in photographs something every cartoonist has drawn for years – a lone man and a girl shipwrecked on this desert island (photos 53–56). I'll admit that this was a set-up story, but it is something that many men would like to happen in their everyday lives. This again is a good example of photo-journalism – it was a challenge from the very first. I was creating a real live adventure just like somebody rowing the Atlantic or sailing a yacht across it.

The idea came one wet, miserable, cold January day while I was travelling up to London by train. I was reading the newspapers, turning over the pages looking for possible picture-stories, when I saw a very funny cartoon of a beautiful girl shipwrecked on a desert island. It immediately set my mind working. I had just been to the Bahamas for a couple of weeks and a friend of mine had taken me on a boat-ride to a very tiny uninhabited island surrounded by blue seas and golden sands fringed with palm trees. He invited me to photograph it then, but as it was it meant nothing photographically. In the very same newspaper that I was reading there was a picture of an attractive semi-naked model girl. The idea hit me then and there – a survival story! After some more deep thought I decided to contact the Special Air Service, who are experts in survival. I told them about my idea and asked them if they would give me a short course in survival. Naturally, I mentioned that I might possibly be accompanied by some glamorous lady. They then readily agreed!

Within no time at all I had telex messages going to the Bahamas setting things up. When I eventually knew the whole idea was feasible I approached the *Sunday Mirror* with a detailed synopsis I had pre-pared, outlining exactly how I saw the story and what would result from it. They immediately saw the possibilities, and within two weeks I was on my way to the Bahamas, accompanied by Julie Ege and Roy Foster (then Art Editor of the *Sunday Mirror*). Roy was coming along to be the contact-man on the radios that would be used in case of emergency, one being on the island with me and one on the main island with Roy. We'd call each other twice a day as a safeguard against accidents. Roy had also helped think out a lot of the photographs we would be doing.

We arrived on the Thursday before the Saturday of the week we would start our stay on the island. There is a tremendous amount of planning in setting up a story such as this, and once you have got the pure administration done, then comes the real head-ache i.e. the photographic side, for you really must visualise most of your pictures beforehand. I suppose it is similar to film-making, knowing in advance the majority of the shots you will want to take, having seen the island and knowing the weather conditions. It also helped knowing what sort of back-drops to expect.

I was by now well acquainted with Julie and had an idea of her impressive personality. With this infor-mation and knowing my own photographic ability I prepared a list of pictures alongside which I noted the equipment I would require for the pictures.

I would be shooting in black and white and in colour and I allowed myself five films per day of each of these. I decide to go for a larger format camera; I would have a $2\frac{1}{4}$ square as my main camera, and I used a Hasselblad. My standard lens for most

pictures would be the 150mm lens, and a second choice of lens would be the normal lens. I had six film magazines, so I could pre-load most of my film each day. I also had two 35mm cameras, a 50mm lens, a 28mm wide angle and a 135mm lens, plus filters – ultra-violet and a three-times yellow filter to fit all lenses. I took three normal professional flashlight outfits (of course working by battery), two reflector umbrellas and stands, a special 30-yard extension lead for flash, a tripod, and a roll of silver paper for reflectors.

Personal items included oil for Julie to put on her skin to give a shiny effect, and a little make-up to help her look cool and glamorous in the heat, for even though we were shipwrecked I could not allow the photographs of my subject to look unattractive. Fortunately, she was an expert at make-up – for the effect of sea water can be quite telling on the face and the skin of any lady – and this was one thing I had to watch. It was for this purpose only that we took along a gallon of water in an old can.

The idea was survival, so we did try collecting water in a plastic sheet, and for our food we caught small fishes and ate palm hearts from the palm trees. Photography itself on the island was limited to certain periods of the day: early morning, late after-noon and evening. In the early morning the light was soft and pleasant, and the sea was that much bluer. At midday, as in all tropical parts of the world, the sun was far too high and very shadowy. We did become fed up and weak from the heat and the lack of food, and we were therefore unable to work flat-out all day. There were times when we had a cool breeze and could work in the shade of the palm trees, which, in fact, was the best place for doing many of our good close-ups.

The palm trees and different vegetation that we found on the island helped to give the impression of a tropical island. Not all the shots were taken in the shade or out in the raging sun; many were taken as night time came on, or as the sun came up. We used the sunset and a fire to give the atmosphere of loneliness in a remote part of the world.

This story was very successful when I got back, and it had produced many good pictures. I shot lots of photographs on this particular assignment as they were needed to illustrate a series that was run for a period of four weeks. Magazines all over the world came after this material and millions of people saw it. This story became a legend and today people still joke and talk about it. I think it must have been one of the most successful glamour stories I have ever done, and I don't believe there are many photographers who specialise in glamour who have done an assignment quite like this!

I would add that Julie and myself did not have one single cross word during our stay on the island and this played a vital part in enabling us to produce good pictures. Bad temper or controversy about what we should or should not shoot would have put a damper on some of our photographs. A good relationship between subject and photographer is important. I believe the photographer is responsible for the creation of a good atmosphere.

I've done other adventure-type glamour stories applying the same photographic technique. I took the former Miss World, Eva Ruber-Staier, across the Kalahari Desert in southern Africa, and top model Jilly Johnson to Barbados for another exotic location (photos 57–59). I much prefer location work to photography in a studio for this reason – lighting, backcloth and atmosphere are in much more abundant supply in natural surroundings.

I do not work more than, say, six times a year in a studio. I do not have one of my own, which means hiring one when necessary, but I do try to keep to the same studio, for even though the strobe lights may be the same as in other studios, each studio has its own characteristics of light reflection. I find that lighting a subject is relatively simple providing you are familiar with the strobes and umbrellas that are required.

I keep to one set-up of lights: a high flash on a boom reflected on to the top of the subject from a silver-coated umbrella, then another high flash in front of the subject slightly to the left of myself and to the right of the subject, at a distance of about three yards from the subject, reflecting the light once again in an umbrella. At times I do fire the flash directly through a white silk umbrella, taking the flash and umbrella back a little and bringing it to the face level of the model. I also use large white reflector boards on either side to capture any light that may be escaping and to reflect it back in.

When working in the studio on fashion or glamour I like to use a $2\frac{1}{4}$ format and work mainly with a Hasselblad equipped with a 150mm lens. If using 35mm cameras then I prefer an 85mm lens. I always use slower films when working on these assignments and usually work with Kodak Plus X in monochrome for better quality. For colour I use a 64 Ektachrome Daylight E6, which can work without filters with daylight-type flash. Apertures are usually f11 for black and white and f8 for colour.

Shooting on location or in the studio, whether it be glamour or fashion, I experiment with lighting,

if time permits, to try to add that something different to the technique, and to expand my knowledge of lighting effects. One set-up I do use quite often on location is that of the flash mounted on a stand and fired straight through a white silk umbrella mounted five to six yards or more from the subject, depending on the strength of the natural light. I use an exposure meter to give the daylight value, and from this judge the strength of the flash required. Remember that the flash is only filling in and giving some lift to the subject against its background. On no account must you over-flash for it produces very amateurish effects; this applies for both black and white and colour.

Nudity, even with an attractive model, can look vulgar if not photographed properly. In my opinion wide-angle lenses must be used with great care, and only when trying to get atmosphere in the photograph. Posing comes naturally to the good model, making the photographer's work that much easier, but he must ensure that she displays no marks on the body caused by tights, bra straps and other tight items of clothing. If possible, advise the model before she comes to the session to leave off such things. Make-up on semi-close-ups must be perfect, as must the hair. Watch for shiny areas that appear on the face, especially after working in a warm studio for a period of time. These usually come under the eyes or on top of the forehead. A dab of light flat make-up will remedy this.

At times when working on location I like to work in soft shade or indoors, using the available window light. Even on the dullest days you can get really good effects. Don't be afraid to use interesting lighting. One such occasion occurred when I had an appointment to photograph the beautiful actress, Gayle Hunnicutt. My appointment had been arranged several weeks beforehand, and Gayle, being a very busy lady, was in and out of the country on film commitments. I had planned to shoot my pictures in nearby Hyde Park, but had to change the plans rapidly due to atrocious weather. I ended up photographing inside her flat by window-lighting (Nos 60 and 61). My exposure was on black and white at 1/15th of a second with the aperture at f3.5 (and on colour at 1/8th of a second at f3.5 and f5.6). Mind you, at times my exposures were going to f2.8 due to the changing light as dark rain clouds passed by outside.

I could not have wished for better results. The pictures were perfect, so don't be too depressed if lighting is not what you had hoped for, but make sure you hold your camera still. I try to avoid using a tripod, for it hinders mobility. Try to find something to steady yourself on. Many photographers use a tripod in their studios, even when working with strobe lighting. I don't know why, for strobe lighting usually fires at very high speeds, and I find a long extension lead from strobes to camera enables me to move round more freely.

Fashion and glamour photography is a lucrative business for those capable of stirring the viewer's imagination. Most newspaper staff photographers try this line of work but find it somewhat more difficult than they imagined. Photographers who are good at this work stay at the top for many years, especially in the fashion field. It's a job they guard with their professional lives. They do have their stormy patches with the whims and changes in the approach of fashion editors who come and go, but on the other hand there is the challenge from their colleagues, ambitious photographers who think they may be able to do better. They are also attracted by the aura that attaches to this field of photography.

What makes a good glamour picture that is usable? First you must remember elementary rules: with nudes, distorted wide-angled pictures are not successful. They may be acceptable for the arty books or magazines, but not newspapers. Newspapers want good quality. The model must also look good, showing clear skin, bright eyes and good teeth and a pleasant smile. Three-quarter lengths are the most popular. Between the waist and knee level is where I usually frame my picture; with a larger image on the negative you get far more impact and quality in the final print. Avoid pulling up from full lengths. If you want more of the body in the picture, and are working for a full length shot, watch the feet; like the hands, if not posed properly they can look ugly. Be careful not to show pubic hair. By using the natural curves of the thighs, or shadows cast by the lights, the full length nude can lose these explicit areas and provide a picture more acceptable for breakfast-table reading.

Backgrounds can be disastrous; there is no excuse for poor backing if shooting in a studio. Watch out for large ugly shadows or dirty marks on the backcloth and, once again, ensure that the body has no marks caused by the clothing.

The impact of fashion photography is obviously helped by the fashion itself; if it is outrageous and very susceptible to photography then it is likely to get more space in the paper than perhaps a tweed suit from an autumn collection. A dress worth thousands of pounds, cut low to the navel, would make space purely on news value and glamour. A photographer who covers fashion needs to develop an awareness of these subtleties even though most of the time he has to make a tweed suit and the like look interesting, for it is the normal clothes that housewife readers buy.

Of course the desert island story is an extreme example of glamour photography, but the principal attitude is there – that of the approach to the subject and the attempt to create something different and adventurous. We must, at the same time, realise that this is pure entertainment for the reader. Forget any ideas that they are buying it for the sake of art. Even though the photographer has used all his artistic talent to make the model look good, and a lot of the effort has come from the photographer to produce the picture, it is still the nudity of the young lady that attracts.

I am of course talking from the reader's viewpoint, and naturally the same would apply to news photographs or, if it comes to that, *any* kind of photography that appears in magazines or newspapers. Readers first look at the event or occasion and then, maybe, consider the photographer.

A picture editor looking at a glamour photograph would do so differently from a reader. I think he must consider equally the standard of glamour and the standard of photography, unlike a news photograph of importance, that can be a little bit down in photographic quality and which he would accept.

The desert island story, on the other hand, was seen by the reader not purely and solely as glamour; to them it was a combination of adventure and glamour, and that was exactly what I wanted to create.

It is worth mentioning the more newsy glamour event, such as a Miss World final, or any beauty contest that has hit the headlines. This is probably where the news photographer gets far more involved than a pure glamour or fashion photographer. I have not been involved in photographing a Miss World final or a beauty contest for several years now, but the techniques are the same.

The active thinkers amongst the photographers do try to come up with something different, but to be honest I don't think they pull it off. The pictures we see each year are either of contestants jumping in the air, the winner bursting into tears as she is proclaimed Miss World, or lying in bed the morning after the contest. For this reason I think they should try for something stronger and more positive. I know the organisers would probably not let one photographer have access to a new Miss World for a complete morning on the following day, but I'm sure if they did it would be a wonderful opportunity to produce something really different.

It's an assignment I would like to do myself and this is how I would tackle such an opportunity. Select the most stunning négligé or other, similar, items of clothing that are very sexy in themselves. This should preferably be in a dark colour, even black, bearing in mind that this picture is not going to show bare breasts or anything like that; it must be in keeping with the title of Miss World.

I would, of course have a studio set up in advance with suitable props – small, elegant things. My choice of camera would be a large format using sheet film for both black and white and colour, the lighting being arranged very naturally. I would be aiming for photographic quality – it must be stunning. I would have standing by a good hairdresser and make-up artist, to create something that's different, not seen by the television viewers or newspapers the night before. I would set the pose, because I prefer landscape (horizontal) shaped photos; they appear to take up more space in a newspaper layout.

The session would take about three hours to shoot, from 9 o'clock to noon. Most of this time would be allowed for make-up and hair. The monochrome prints would be 20 x 16 inches and would be processed and finished by three in the afternoon, in time for any newspaper to spread it and give a real quality approach to a Miss World. I know with confidence that this picture would publish widely, and here, I feel, is the way many of us think out a major picture spread; all you need is a little co-operation.

53–56. Glamour on a Desert Island

Setting up a glamour/adventure picture series can
cause more headaches than one might imagine. You
must get your photographic equipment right for the
job, first of all; with glamour you need treble the
amount normally carried. On arriving at your location
work out a timetable – to make use of early-morning
and late-evening light – and look for locations at the
same time noting what the light is like.

The setting was an uninhabited island in the
Bahamas. Technically it was a photographic challenge.
With the varying lighting conditions, the early morning
proved the best time for pure glamour, the soft light
allowing 1/250 second at f8 on Plus X, with not too
much contrast between highlighting and shadows.
The early afternoon light with sun reflecting back
into the palm trees' shade was intriguing, suggesting
1/125 second at f8 on Plus X, using the 150mm lens
on a hand-held Hasselblad for semi and close-up shots.

The evening photograph (No 56) against the setting
sun was taken on 35mm camera with a 35mm lens,
the speed being 1/15 second at f11 with a direct
flash some six yards away on an extension lead and
using a yellow filter.

I think credit for the success of my desert island
picture feature must go to Julie Ege herself. She
adapted overnight from a comfortable London
existence to survival on a desert island. She made no
complicated preparations for the pictures – many
women can take hours before they are made up to their
satisfaction for the camera, but Julie was ready in
minutes. I believe Julie led the way for the good
quality glamour that appears in many of today's daily
newspapers.

On this assignment my camera equipment was a
Hasselblad, three 35mm cameras, 35mm, 50mm,
135mm and a 300mm lenses, three flash outfits, two
umbrellas, a tripod, plastic bags to keep the cameras
protected from the sand, dusters and dusting brush,
rolls of silver paper for reflecting light, and two
portable radios for emergency use.

I was also very careful to unload film in subdued
light, and then to pack the films away into the coolest
spot available.

78

56

57–59. Jilly Johnson in Barbados

During the winter months photographers try to find sunny and warm backgrounds for glamour pictures – which proves very difficult in this country! For these pictures I took model girl Jilly Johnson to Barbados. Not wanting to have only glamour photographs – nude girl on beach, nude girl under palm trees, and so on – I varied my pictures to give the widest possible scope for future use of the material.

The glamour shot (No 57) was used purely as light relief on a front page, the close-up (No 58) was used as a poster by a newspaper, and the shot under the palm trees (No 59) was used in colour to illustrate holiday features.

As with all glamour assignments particularly those abroad, I carry more equipment than at any other time. All three pictures were taken on a Hasselblad fitted with a 150mm lens; the film, Kodak Plus X.

The nude picture I shot 1/250 second at f8 on black and white. The light on this picture was made very difficult by strong back-lighting reflecting on the sand.

The close-up was taken with the aid of a white sheet acting as a reflector board; the exposure for this was 1/125 second at f8.

For the palm tree picture I used a three-times yellow filter and worked with a shutter speed of 1/250 second at f11.

60

62

60–62. Gayle Hunnicutt

Nos 60 & 61 were taken by natural window light with outside stormclouds reducing the light occasionally, so the exposures varied from frame to frame.

Gayle's features have a classical elegance. She has an exceptional type of beauty to be captured by the camera and natural lighting helped me to do just this. Originally it was to have been photographed in the open on location, so with limited flash equipment available I decided to make do with the existing light. If strobe lighting had been at hand I would have used it. I know that flash, even if it had been bounced, would not have produced the moodiness in the pictures that the natural light gave.

Using a 35mm camera the shutter speed varied from 1/15 second to 1/8 second, with apertures ranging from f3.5 to f5.6, the camera being held quite still. The through camera metering was perfect on this occasion – no glaring light that could cause a misreading.

The third photograph of Miss Hunnicutt and son Nolan (No 62) was taken on a different occasion but under similar lighting conditions, except that this was outside. The lens was a 105mm, the aperture f4, at a shutter speed of 1/250 second on 35mm Tri X film.

63 & 64. Simple Fashions

Actress Joan Collins models dresses designed by
Thea Porter. These pictures are not for the high
fashion magazines such as *Vogue ;* they were kept
simple and clean photographically, with the intention
of not losing detail, so as to make good blocks for
newspaper reproduction.

The indoor shot (No 63) I managed to get away
with in two respects – the right hand is only just
acceptable being far too much out of picture to the
left; secondly, if the picture had been any more
cluttered up I would have lost Miss Collins and the
dress she was wearing. In this picture I think the
mirror helped to convey a busy effect.

The photograph was taken on a 2¼ square Rolleiflex
camera, the lighting was with umbrella and flash
bounced from it, the aperture was f11 on Plus X film.

The outside picture (No 64) is also simple. I used
a flash fired directly through a white umbrella, at the
subject and positioned at shoulder height. The
distance of flash to subject was 10 feet and camera
from subject around 6 feet. The actual picture takes
up nearly the full negative, which saved loss of quality
in enlarging. The reason I used a fill-in flash for the
outdoor shot was that if I had taken my picture by
the dull available light the photographs would have
looked flat and not in keeping with the fashion; the
flash also helped lift out the design of the fashion.

The camera was a Rolleiflex, working at a shutter
speed of a 1/60 second (to allow for picking up spare
daylight) at an aperture of f8.

65. Anazette Chase

Many a time it is difficult to find a simple plain background when working on location; plain walls can be uninteresting and the subjects do not always come over as being relaxed when they're just sitting in a chair.

This picture of American actress Anazette Chase was taken in a room in the Beverley Wiltshire hotel in Los Angeles. I had been invited by film producer John Marshall to photograph Miss Chase as she was playing a leading role with Muhammad Ali in the film 'The Greatest' which was about Ali's own life. Wanting to make the pictures a little different, I asked her to lie on the floor in a pool of natural light coming through the window, and to adjust her hair and dress to give a suggestion of movement.

The picture was taken on a 28mm lens using a 35mm camera. The aperture was f8 at a speed of 1/30 second.

66. Barbara Carrera

Actress Barbara Carrera was a photographer's dream to photograph (she was one of the world's top models). Her poses came easily during a break in filming 'Masada', in Israel. The picture was taken by a 35mm camera fitted with a 28mm lens and a three-times yellow filter, at a speed of 1/250 on HP5 film at f11.

67. Penthouse Pet

This young lady was chosen by *Penthouse* magazine
as Penthouse Pet of the Year. It was one of a series I
shot on location at Longleat, the stately home of
Lord Bath.

Using one of the large beds for the model to pose
on, I worked with natural light from the window.
The 35mm camera was fitted with a 28mm lens using
a shutter speed of 1/30 second at f5.6 on Tri X film.

68. Kerry Lou Bayliss

I chose Kerry Lou Bayliss as the new face of 1978 – a
fortunate choice as her subsequent career proved.
The lighting for both black and white and colour was
perfect; I was using one silver-backed umbrella and
bouncing flash into it, reflecting from a distance of
10 feet at a height of 8 feet, offset to the left of subject.
On the right a large white reflector board helped to
catch wasted light and reflected it back onto subject.
I also used a bounced flash on a boom directly over
the subject, which gave an even overall light that
gave some lift of the subject from background.

Looking at this picture afterwards I realised I had
made a mistake, something I should have spotted
when posing my subject. I am usually very careful

about hands, but here the hand resting on the table is
badly placed – I should have made sure I used the
full beauty of the hands showing the fingers. Kerry
has very dark hair and to offset this a little I purchased
a pair of pale blue leotards to make a stunning colour
contrast.

The camera was a Hasselblad with a 150mm lens,
the film Plus X and the exposure 1/250 second at f11.

91

69 & 70. A Bond Girl

Barbara Bach, who starred in the James Bond film 'The Spy Who Loved Me', was photographed in a garden in Rome. I wanted to avoid shooting in a studio, but at the same time have a background that was placeless. The garden itself offered no decent background, but I needed privacy for the glamour shots that I wanted to take. Attempting these in the street would have caused a riot. It took some time to clear empty bottles and rubbish to create the picture area with a simple background, and it was helped by the strong backlight.

The hatless photograph (No 69) in fact had a wire fence in the background that I could do little about, except work at an aperture of f5.6 on a 300mm lens with a speed setting of 1/250 second. The photograph with the hat (No 70) was taken on an 85mm lens, also at f5.6 at 1/250 second.

7 News Photography

The best way I can describe news photography is that it's like a wonderful Irish stew – all the ingredients imaginable are thrown in! You will witness the bizarre and the tragic. It is probably the epitome of photo-journalism, covering a war on one assignment and photographing an irascible politician the next. Or it might be a film star who objects to having pictures taken! A news photographer's everyday assignments will range from a Miss World contest to a Football or Rugby final – a train or plane crash to a baby show. This is my kind of photography; absurd, frustrating and exciting. Over the years, I've had the good fortune to travel to most countries of the world. There was a time when I planned to give it all up when I reached the age of fifty, but today, not feeling a day older than when I started, I'm looking forward to the next forty-odd years.

For this zest for life I thank news photography. I've been talking about the need to be compact and mobile and always at the ready. This must apply that much more to the news photographer. The equipment carried on an assignment is fairly universal; makes of cameras may be different, but the actual contents of the camera bags are the same except for the film stock. If you are with a magazine you must carry more colour; if you are just covering for newspapers then obviously more black and white.

The big assignments come right out of the blue. A flash news item on the tapes can start the whole force of the world's photographic and news media rolling. Decisions are made in minutes. A photographer covering a press reception at the Savoy, maybe enjoying his first gin and tonic of the day and looking forward to going out with his wife that evening, can find himself two hours later being borne in a large Jumbo jet to a destination in far-off Africa or India. Events happen fast. A short time later he's probably still cradling a gin and tonic, but put there by an air stewardess. His mind will be alert, planning for the unexpected. Already armed with a flight timetable, he will be looking for times of aircraft on which he could probably ship his first material back home. He will be accompanied by a journalist colleague from his own or other newspapers. Their enthusiasm and alarming conversation will interest other passengers. There is a tremendous comradeship and friendship between the world's Press, but the competition is fierce. Once at their journey's end they split into small groups, taking taxis either to their hotels or ministries. If it's a war, the more adventurous will have a go at getting to the front line.

I will use one of my war stories to give some impression of what happens to the photo-journalist who is responsible for covering world events. This is by no means the most sensational or memorable war assignment I've covered, but it is the everyday problem we must expect if we undertake these assignments, and it's just one of many that has happened to me. It all started early one Monday morning when I was seated in the armchair at our office reading the morning papers, when on the nine o'clock news there was a news flash that President Makarios of Cyprus was believed to have been assassinated and that fighting had broken out in Cyprus. This was yet another part of the world I knew like the back of my hand; only two weeks before I had been photographing the President in his palace in Nicosia for a special session (photo 71).

Quickly checking my equipment and putting some more films in my camera bag, I was on my way to the airport. My partner was already making flight reservations on the 11 o'clock Middle East flight to Beirut, but had no more news of the situation by the time I had taken off. Four and a half hours later I arrived in Beirut and made straight for the Palm Beach Hotel, for I knew that this would be the best place to contact other foreign correspondents who work the Middle East area. (This is another small point to bear in mind; it's vital to know where you are going when you get off that aircraft!)

Within minutes of arriving at the hotel I had met my old friend Don Wise, then chief foreign correspondent of the *Daily Mirror*, who was based in Beirut. Within a short time we were joined by other correspondents and newspapermen who were pouring in from all around the world, all unable to get out of Beirut to Cyprus as all the airports and ports were still closed there. For photographers it was a little depressing to know that a day had been wasted, and for a photographer that can be disastrous – as each hour goes by, news can get stale. The reporters, at least were able to pick up some news from Cyprus Radio that came over loud and clear in Beirut. It is this sort of frustrating situation a photographer must learn to live with and not panic about. I'm glad to say there were photo-journalists arriving all the time, so by that evening I did have others sharing the same situation. We had also learned from Cyprus Radio that Archbishop Makarios was still alive and in hiding in the mountain area, so this made it more vital that we got to Cyprus as soon as possible.

Next morning I was up at dawn and decided with Don Wise to search high and low to find a way of getting across the short stretch of the Mediterranean to Cyprus. Knowing that flying was an impossibility (the Lebanese Government do not allow private charter aircraft to operate), Don went to try the harbour club where the luxury yachts were moored, while I went to the dockyard accompanied by photographer Harry Dempster of the *Daily Express*. Our job was to try to find anyone who, for a reasonable sum, would take us across. It was very difficult trying to find a small boat to take us on. Our reception was rude and very aggressive, presumably because they did not want to show that they were afraid of such a journey. It was still early morning when we found a portly, unshaven Egyptian skipper who had a very dilapidated cargo boat laden with timber. Surprisingly, he agreed to unload his cargo but explained that it would take all day, that he would not be able to sail until that evening and the fee would be £4500. Whether he expected us to accept this I never found out – for I just said 'Yes' and agreed to meet him later that afternoon to hand over the money. Need I say that finding £4500 at short notice was no small commitment; at the time I had just over £200 in my pocket.

In some haste I rang all the hotels and bars, the best contact points for any journalists who might be interested in taking a share in the boat hire. Harry also took off to round up as many passengers as possible for what seemed a most unlikely voyage. Rumour had gone round that any boat attempting to dock would be fired on by the Cypriots. I'll never forget that afternoon with the skipper, in a small, hot, smelly office alongside the quay of Beirut harbour, taking money from other newspapermen who by then had agreed to come; in fact we did such a good business that I got a £20 discount on my ticket!

We sailed that evening just before dusk, after loading food supplies and our baggage, colliding with another boat and destroying part of its bridge as we left the harbour. Some may have thought this was a bad omen, but none of us was particularly worried. We spent the night lying in the open on the deck of the cargo holds, the only place to sleep on board. Next morning we were flying the Egyptian flag as we sailed on a very blue sea into the mouth of Famagusta harbour. The place had an uncanny air, not a movement in the brilliant sunshine of that mid-morning. Several of our colleagues were gathered around the wireless operator trying to make contact with the Cypriot officials. All we photographers were on deck, armed with cameras and waiting for something to happen. On these occasions you seem to be always peering through the viewfinder. We were soon told not to move, that someone would be getting in touch with us.

Three very hot hours later, a small boarding party came on board to greet us on behalf of the new President of Cyprus, Nicos Sampson, the man who had once been sentenced to death by the British Government for his part in killings and terrorist attacks. I'd met Sampson several times during the years I'd covered Cyprus in the 1950s troubles. It seemed ironic that Sampson had set himself up as President; in the early days he was supposed to be a newspaperman. Surrounded with cameras and typewriters and television equipment, we must have seemed a strange party as we went ashore later that afternoon, yet again to be frustrated, for they marshalled us into a luxury hotel under guard for the night as their 'guests' and told us that the next morning we would meet the President.

No matter how experienced a photo-journalist may be, the tension and physical strain of trying to get on to an assignment builds up. Next morning, it proved just too much for Harry Dempster and myself, and maybe we were a little foolhardy. We talked to a young English couple on holiday in Cyprus – they just wanted to get off the island – to let us escort them to the airport as we had heard that a plane would leave for London later that day. They had a small hired Mini Moke car, discreetly loaded with all their baggage for fear the authorities would see that they were intending to take off. We got under way for

1 Out of the bunker

There are photographic secrets and obviously I'm going to keep a few. Many people have asked me how I shot this photograph of a golfer getting out of a bunker – it shows the sand exploding towards the camera and the golf ball motionless. It is not a composite; the ball is genuinely in the photograph and it was not taken on a motor drive camera.

I used a flash fired through an umbrella to clean up the shadows. The picture was taken with a 35mm camera fitted with a 21mm lens, on 64 A.S.A. Ektachrome film. The shutter speed was 1/60 second at an aperture of f16. I used a 1/60 second for synchronization with flash and to allow plenty of stop (aperture) to give me depth . . . simple!

2 Telly Savalas

A picture of the world's most famous bald head. The portrait was taken on a Hasselblad fitted with a normal lens; the film was 64 A.S.A. Ektachrome daylight 120, hand held for a 1/30 second at f5.6. It was taken by natural lighting in his caravan on a film set in Hollywood.

3 The Saint of Calcutta

Mother Theresa is one of the greatest women I have ever photographed. This impression I had in 1969 when I photographed her for the first time, and it remains my conviction today. This kind, gentle lady, with blue, deep-set eyes that look into one's soul as she speaks, has dedicated her life to the destitute and dying in the slums of Calcutta, babies left lying unwanted in the gutters and lepers with terrible deformities. She cares for them, holds their hands and tends their wounds, as well as travelling the world to raise funds to support her home for them. Her 1979 Nobel Peace Prize was a just tribute to her work.

I spent several days photographing her at work. A photographer working in the slums of Calcutta finds it difficult and at times dangerous. You are unwelcome to the masses and if seen with a camera attract hostile crowds. The presence of Mother Theresa did help, but at times I found it advisable to stay in her rickety and battered old Mini van as she made her rounds to collect the unwanted babies.

Once a week she goes to visit her home for the destitute and dying that lies in the heart of Calcutta's poorest area. Here she talks with and comforts the poor wretches who live in the city's gutters. Those desperately ill she takes into her home, a large single-storey building which dates from the era of the British Raj. Its tall, glassless windows are the only means of ventilation and light, and admit the noise and chatter of the streets outside.

To be discreet and avoid attracting attention I used only one 35mm camera fitted with a 28mm lens, and in my pocket had a 35mm and 105mm lens with a couple of rolls of spare colour film. My commission for this subject specified all colour on 64 A.S.A. Ektachrome only, despite its unsuitability for the majority of the photographs – the light was extremely bad for interiors, as in the 'House of Death', my title for this particular scene. Here the exposure was 1/8 second at f3.5. Some may have been tempted to use flash but I felt that the dark shadows and the pools of light given by the high window helped to create the atmosphere this tragic scene required, even though the darkness hid some unpleasant scenes.

Nicosia. It was calm in a kind of uneasy peace that literally smelt of death. Having successfully seen the young couple off to safety, we booked into the Ledra Palace Hotel, then headed for the area around the President's palace. We soon realised that this was where the heart of the fighting had taken place; the area was devastated. We were about to take some pictures but a lone soldier looking very tense and pointing an automatic decided otherwise and ordered us away from the area.

It was now over 48 hours since I had left London, and I had taken few pictures of significance for the big story that was taking over the headlines all over the world. The writers had something to report – they were making space in their newspapers with eye-witness accounts of events that happened before we had left London, and there was the whole political situation to be reported. Words, but not pictures. I was beginning to feel uneasy because of the lack of results. For the enormous trouble we had put in just getting to Cyprus, it seemed hardly worth it. Harry and I returned to the hotel to find other colleagues catching up with us.

We were informed that the press conference with Sampson was definitely on for around two o'clock that afternoon. I was also fortunate enough to learn that a flight direct to London was going that afternoon at around four-thirty, the first since the troubles had started. This is where the thinking ahead comes in, for I knew that there could be trouble in trying to wire my pictures to London. Communications were becoming bogged down, not only by the results of the past few days' troubles, but also by the large number of journalists arriving who would take up many of the lines out. There were about 350 of us already on the island, so I made plans to air-freight my films, contacting British Airways' shipping office at the airport before I went off to the Press conference. Time was in my favour: Nicosia was two hours ahead of London. Flying time between Nicosia and London was about four hours, so this meant my films would be back in London at around seven o'clock that evening with luck. It was cutting things fine for editions, but there was really no alternative, so I decided to take the gamble and use air-freight.

The Press conference was more like a circus and, as is usual with all press conferences, started late. This one did not start until well after three o'clock, causing me more anxious moments, for I had to be at the airport three-quarters of an hour before the aircraft took off if I was to ship my films. Sampson did his part, showing off whips and other weapons that the Makarios police had allegedly used to torture prisoners. I shot black and white and colour, one roll on each, using Tungsten film, as they had plenty of television lights illuminating our subjects (see photo 72). The drive from the Press conference to Nicosia airport must have taken my fastest driving, but luckily there were no police operating because of the chaotic situation. The packet did arrive in London at the time I expected and made the late editions of the *Daily Mail* and *Daily Telegraph*.

The following morning the whole of the Press corps was rounded up for a tour of the battle areas which Harry and myself had tried to photograph the day before, but this was now a complete waste of time so far as I was concerned. Having hired my own transport, a small Mini, I decided to drive to Kyrenia, a small, picturesque harbour facing the Turkish mainland. All through the Cyprus troubles we had said that if the Turks ever invaded, this would be their landfall. This urge to go to Kyrenia must have been the second sense one seems to develop over the years in this business. It's uncanny, but sometimes you know the exact place where something is going to happen. I went equipped for what was supposed to be a quick look-see, to have a quiet lunch and then to return to Nicosia and rejoin the press group. But after lunch I had this strong feeling that I should remain overnight. That afternoon I spent my time checking out the spot where an invasion could take place.

I booked in at the Dolphin Hotel, noting that there was a small United Nations post right in front of it. Next morning I woke at 4.30 and looked out to sea through the mist. I saw a faint shape of a warship, the flash of a signal lamp to another ship, then more war vessels appeared. It was as I had guessed: an invasion was about to take place. I was in the right place at the right time with no competition, although there were over 300 other newspapermen on the island. All the frustrations and hard work of the past few days had paid off – or so it seemed, for I was soon pinned down by Turkish jet fighters bombing and strafing with rockets. Colour photo No 5 is one of the shots I managed to take. I phoned Nicosia early that Saturday morning to contact chief reporter Brian Parks of the *Daily Mail*, for the *Daily Mail* was one of my commissions for this assignment. He said Nicosia was quiet; not a sound to be heard. He took off in a taxi to join me in what turned out to be another series of hair-raising events that are another story in themselves. This is not a book of personal experiences, but all this illustrates what sort of thing can go into getting a news photograph. It's impossible to give this atmosphere of creative photography in long-winded technical details. A photograph taken at f8 is a photograph taken at f8, 1/250th of a second is a flash of light. In this story the emphasis was on techniques rather than creativity.

I am sure professional and amateur photographers alike know the feeling of excitement in the build-up to taking a photograph, whether at the Farnborough Air Show or at a wedding. For a news photographer these feelings are intensified a thousand times. The occasion itself, even without thinking about pictures, can put a tremendous strain on one's energy. Spread over several days, as in the Cyprus conflict, this tension leaves me exhausted, but when the finale comes up the adrenalin soon flows – once again I was refreshed with excitement of the moment.

Little did I know then that I'd have more and greater disappointments and would be denied my scoop, for I was eventually pinned down by the fighting, and it was not till four days later that I was rescued by the British Navy. Within hours I was flown back to London on an R.A.F. VC10 and arrived in Fleet Street in exactly the same clothes in which I had lunched at Kyrenia, unwashed and unshaven. I realised my pictures had become historic without the news value they would have had if I could have got them out within the day, or even thirty-six hours after I had taken them. Their only value was for a spread as a 'diary' in the *Daily Mail* – events as they had happened. The pictures are now in my library as a permanent record of the events of that week. This should, of course, have been a world scoop had I not been pinned down. So it is with these ups and downs that the news photographer lives his life, walking on a tight rope, but it is a life I know none of us would change for anything else.

71. Archbishop Makarios

The scene in the Presidential Palace, Nicosia, as Archbishop Makarios takes a leisurely stroll to his office. Little did I know that two weeks later this very palace would be destroyed during heavy fighting, the Archbishop narrowly escaping an assassination attempt and fleeing to the hills for safety. When I talk of freezing a moment of time, this picture illustrates just that. It was one of the last photographs taken of Makarios in the Palace.

The 35mm Olympus camera was fitted with a 28mm lens, the shutter speed was 1/250 second with the aperture at f8, the film Kodak Tri X.

72. Nicos Sampson

Not one of my sharpest pictures, due to the fact that it was taken on a 300mm lens at a crowded Press conference in Nicosia during the Cyprus problems. Hand-held, it was taken at 1/60 second with an aperture of f5.6. I chose to work by natural light on this particular occasion – flash would have meant getting closer, and as Sampson was sitting on a stage it would have increased the upward angle, causing the microphone to cover his face. The camera was a 35mm.

73. Pacific Glory

This photograph of an oil-tanker on fire after a
collision in the English Channel was taken from a
small aircraft. I find that for air to ground photography
it is best to avoid shooting through the aircraft
window. With most small charter aircraft it is usually
possible to take off the door or open a window before
take-off, to give better vision in both directions from
the aircraft; this also cuts out possible reflections from
perspex. The larger format camera would give better
detail but the 35mm camera affords you much more
versatility with long focus lenses. I have at times used
as long a lens as 500mm to shoot from an aircraft.
If conditions are good, some quality can be gained by
the use of filters, as in this photograph, which adds
some cloud detail.

This picture was taken on a 28mm lens with a shutter
speed of 1/500 second at f8, using a three-times yellow
filter. I use the through-the-lens metering system
on this type of photograph, but always make sure
I expose ½ to 1 stop under. The film was Kodak Tri X.

74. Premier Trudeau

Often when covering one story you will run into
another. Here, for example, I had been covering the
Queen's tour of Canada and it was after her departure
when Premier Trudeau, who had been seeing Her
Majesty away, called his children from behind a line
of dignitaries. The military band was still playing as
the guard of honour was marching off – as for most
children, the occasion was very exciting for them and
they marched up and down ignoring their father's
pleas to leave quietly with him.

The photograph was taken with a 300mm lens at
1/250 second at an aperture of f8.

8 Features

In photo-journalism there is an overlap between all branches. For instance, certain set-up sports pictures become features, and glamour and fashion pictures have a feature style about them. Any photo-journalist specialising in one particular field, whether it be sport, Royalty, crime or whatever, will at times get involved in feature pictures, as does the news-photographer who covers hard news stories. This happened to me recently in Kenya at the funeral of President Kenyatta.

There were plenty of good news pictures to be taken, but my strongest picture was of a small white boy on the shoulders of his father in a vast black African crowd (photo 76). I saw immediately the potential of this picture, for it summed up what the African situation is all about. A lone white face lost in a crowd, proving the point that people of all races can live together and could come to pay homage to their President. Also, because of the contrast of skin colours it was perfect for black and white photography. I had to take great care not to show the boy's father, for another white face would have lost the feeling of isolation of that small boy. At the same time, the young lad was totally acceptable to all. This I would class as a pure feature picture rather than a hard news story.

Then there is the 'in-depth' feature – a series of pictures that tell a story about one particular subject. I've already said that the days of the long-winded picture feature are past, but I still undertake the more in-depth story, not only for personal satisfaction but also to cater for the remaining magazines that require the longer article. You must also remember that the picture editor does like to have a certain amount of selection, but even major features in magazines today come down to four or six pages, which really does give little space for a major picture spread.

One such story feature I undertook in 1969; it was a long walk of some 200 miles into the Himalayas. The walk took me near the Tibetan border, and the actual assignment was to find the old Gurkha soldiers who had served with the British Army (photos 78–81). With two Sherpas and one guide, the journey proved to be a photographer's dream. I met people in remote mountain areas which few white men had ever visited before, encounters of mutual curiosity, and each day a new landscape would unfold to provide a new photographic challenge.

For the journey I carried in my back pack three 35mm cameras and the usual range of lenses up to 300mm, a selection of yellow filters, as well as u.v. filters for colour photography to help cut down the predominant ultra-violet light. Here again, the best time for taking photographs was either early morning or late evening. It's strange how landscapes seem to attract a photographer; they throw out a challenge to the photographer with a keen eye for a feature picture. For most of the landscape photos I used a 28mm lens on a 35mm camera, almost invariably loading the camera with Tri X black and white film, and of course shooting with a yellow filter. For colour, depending on the lighting conditions, I had a choice of films. I had either a fast or slightly slower Extachrome, or Kodachrome when light was strong.

I always used a u.v. filter to cut out the blue effect in these high altitudes. Filters should be used more often by the average photographer; I think landscape photography is an area in which we are allowed some latitude, where filters can give the photograph more effect. For the good still picture you must condense all the atmosphere onto that one frame, you must capture the mood of the moment, and here in the Himalayas the black and white pictures were helped tremendously by the use of the yellow filter.

One in-depth feature assignment that I covered a couple of years ago was the legendary Loch Ness monster which, whether one believes in it or not, has tremendous fascination for millions the world over. Before leaving London I had already planned my main pictures, knowing that I stood very little chance of photographing Nessie herself; I should point out that, as far as the truth about whether the monster existed or not was concerned, I went with a completely open mind. Now, after my time there, I believe there is something in the story, bearing in mind the interviews I had with respectable and intelligent local people. It was my genuine belief and curiosity that helped me take reasonably good photographs on the subject of something that was not making itself visible. All I had was landscapes. If I had gone with an attitude of disbelief I think my photographs would have been uninteresting.

I decided to use the loch's beauty for my impact pictures; even though I had not seen the place beforehand I had a mental picture of it, and it did live up to my expectations, even allowing for the mid-winter season. It took about a week to produce all the photographs. For the first couple of days I drove many miles around the loch taking the odd picture with changing light and changing weather from early morning to late night, using a three-times yellow filter to bring out the clouds and punch more atmosphere into what could have been a very plain landscape. On all these pictures I worked at a slow shutter speed of 1/15 second with a hand-held camera, enabling me to stop right down to f16.

In between times I had started fixing appointments with local people who claimed definitely to have seen the monster. As I have said, they were very respectable people – a district nurse, a priest and a water bailiff who had worked on the loch all his life and on several occasions had seen the monster at close quarters.

When photographing these people I did not use a flash as on other occasions (when I need to help balance the light between subject and background); this time I chose to work with straight daylight even though it was very dull. A flash would have taken away that certain bleakness.

The actual feature when completed was about 25 pictures in all, in both black and white and colour. These included aerial shots of the loch, for I wanted to give a real impression of the loch itself. Words also came easily for the text of this particular story, there were plenty of facts, figures and interviews. It was photographically rewarding, enjoyable in all ways and made more satisfying by the fact that it published very well internationally. It goes to show that a positive approach and a new look at an old story can be very well worthwhile (see photos 82–4).

Another photograph of a landscape that particularly pleased me was a photograph on an assignment in Northern Ireland – yes, a landscape, but very much a feature picture (No 92). It was a scene half-way between Belfast and Londonderry – a stone painted with political graffiti. To me it stood out like a sore thumb, against a dramatic sky. Captured in black and white, it was a picture made more dramatic by my use of filters – and by my request to the darkroom to print it well up.

An action sports picture is pure sport, but take the sports personality away from the sporting surrounding and you create a sports feature picture. I have done this with champion jockeys Lester Piggott and Pat Eddery. Lester Piggott I photographed in the Bahamas, getting fit for a new racing season (photo 12). I used a personality against a landscape, and because he is a sporting personality it must be a sports feature picture. The photograph of Pat Eddery the day after he won the jockey championship (photo 13) is simple, yet also very marketable. Here I also used landscape and a personality to produce a semi-portrait, and again this must be considered as a feature photograph. The news photographer's work overlaps into other areas, and this applies even more so to the feature photographer, for he must visualise what is unseen to many of us in all fields. It is his eye and brain that brings out the photographic idea and then puts it into print.

Feature pictures of most human interest subjects can be timeless. If you are undertaking such stories remember that it is more profitable over a period and more valuable for your library if the shot is of international interest, especially those of people who are world famous. A news-type feature is more often than not of value at the time only. I have brought three group photographs into this section, for they are photographs of what was happening at the time and today hold a limited library value.

Group photographs have always held a fascination for me. There is the unknown; When it was it taken? Who are they? What do the details of dress indicate? What was the exact period in time? Even more interesting, I think, are old pictures of groups of people. Are they related to any living person? After a few generations have passed is there still somebody alive who really is the living image of someone of years gone by? A good example of this is our Royal Family. They have been photographed more than most over the years, so it is easy to compare the older photographs with today's.

I suppose I've become known for taking group photographs to illustrate certain types of stories. I would like to give you some idea of my thinking when producing one of these group pictures. The same technique could be applied to a family group, making the photograph much more interesting and at the same time creating a permanent record for the family album. Firstly, organise everyone concerned, placing them in some order. Endeavour to keep everyone interested, because if someone at the back feels left out he or she can completely spoil the picture, and they are indeed as important as any other. Everyone must look straight at the camera, their expressions suiting the occasion. If the group is spread out over a depth of several yards from front to back, I find a slow speed with plenty of stop (aperture) is required to give a reasonable depth of focus, so I focus on the person nearest the camera. I separate the subjects so that each becomes an interesting and individual unit within the group. Of course this is not always possible due to limited space, as with the army at Crossmaglen (photo 94), but if it is possible find a good location with a simple background. A picturesque background can help not only to improve the picture photographically but, for picture journalism, can also act as part of the story.

These photographs (Nos 97-9) are typical of the groups I most enjoy taking. No 97 shows the Chief Constable of Surrey, Mr P. Matthews, with members of the Surrey Police. This took a little time to set up, getting together all the people concerned from among those responsible for fighting crime, from the Accident Unit and Murder Squad to the Bobby on the beat. The idea came after reading a report on policemen's pay and conditions being debated in Parliament at the time. I knew the right photograph would be interesting and bring home to the public just how great a part the police play in our everyday lives. In fact several days before I had had the idea, I noticed our village Bobby was once again riding a bike and learnt the reason for this – to get policemen back on the beat (in other words, out of the car) to re-establish better communications with the public. It gave me food for thought. I had to have something with impact, which is why I decided on the group picture of the Chief Constable and representatives of his police force. The location had to be right. Surrey being the Stockbroker belt, the picture would have looked out of character taken in the backyard of a Police Station, so I chose a typical Surrey village

with a duck pond. I took the photograph on a $2\frac{1}{4}$ square camera using a 55mm lens on Plus X at 1/125 second at f11.

In the photograph I had the Chief Constable and village policeman equally prominent, with the more glamorous units filling out the rest of the picture.

Another location for a group photograph was in the charming village of Shere, chosen because of its picturesque character and because it's not very far from my home. One of my colleagues and I worked together on this idea during a coalminers' strike when the country was going through a very bad time. My colleague had in mind a series of pictures of people from different walks of life with their comments about the situation put together with an 'England expects' theme. After some discussion I suggested taking a typical English village and photographing its core inhabitants – the butcher, baker, policeman, blacksmith, farm-labourer, doctor, publican and so on. Explaining our idea to them all was arranged, and they were very helpful in producing this picture; they really did have strong feelings about the state of the country.

I shot the photograph (No 98) in the mid-morning on a Sunday in the village square. The weather was dull and overcast, so I worked at an exposure of 1/15 second at f11, using a 35mm camera as it is much easier to hold still than a larger format. The lens was a 28mm and the film was Tri X.

The next scene was many miles away from Shere; it was in San Francisco for a group photograph of the city's murder squad (No 99). This picture was based on Perry Mason and other TV detectives who have made the city's crimebusters famous. I spent the best part of a week with them and with an undercover unit; this shot was the main photograph of the series, showing the chief of detectives in the foreground with members of his squad in their office. San Francisco itself would have offered a far better background for such a picture but, due to bad weather, the office it had to be. Also, I wanted their jackets off to show the guns.

This picture was taken on a $2\frac{1}{4}$ square Hasselblad on Plus X film with bounced flash; the lens was a 55mm with an aperture of f5.6 at 1/60 second.

75-77. Kenyatta's Funeral

This is only part of an overall scene of thousands of
people outside the State House in Nairobi, as they
waited to pay their last respects to President Jomo
Kenyatta after his death.

Out in the crowd, about thirty yards from me, was
a little white boy on the shoulders of his father. I was
using a 75–150mm zoom lens which is ideal in these
situations, working at a shutter speed of 1/250 second
at f8, which enabled me to get pleasing results in both
black and white and colour. In this type of lighting
condition I make sure not to underexpose. The
picture is semi-back-lit and underexposure would have
lost considerable detail in the black faces. I deliberately
did not show the boy's father, waiting for him to be
concealed by the crowd, for if he had been included
the photograph would have been less meaningful;
photographed this way I was able to get across the
message that black and white can live together.

For the picture of President Kenyatta laying in
state (No 75) I again used the 75–150mm zoom lens

at a speed of 1/60 second, the same scene being lit by
television lights.

The close-up of his wife at the funeral (No 77) was
also on the zoom at 1/250 second at f5.6.

107

78–81. A Walk in the Himalayas

My Himalayan walk is one of my most memorable assignments. The story itself had little, if any, news value; I would put it into the same category as a feature assignment, not limited to a particular date. Even today, the pictures taken on this walk are still being published.

I first visited Nepal in the early Sixties. At that time it was untouched by the commercialism of tourist package holidays and the like; Katmandu's international airport was just a dusty runway and the largest aircraft able to land there was the old Dakota. It was then still a very primitive country, full of beautiful landscapes and friendly people. I suppose this is what must have attracted me to this strange part of the world. It was in 1969, on my fourth visit to Nepal, that I eventually got my small expedition under way, the idea being to find ex-Gurkha soldiers, especially the three (then) living holders of the Victoria Cross in a remote mountain area below the Himalayas.

With the help of the British Army who recruit these diminutive but fierce men into their ranks, I set out from the town of Tansing with two Gurkha tribal porters and one English-speaking guide. The walk was to take me into the remote areas where very few white men had travelled before, right up near the Tibetan borders and under the snow-swept peaks of Annapurna and Dhaulagiri. My Sherpas carried our tent, bedding and a few essential foods, including spices that would help make the food we bought *en route* more palatable. I carried personal equipment, cameras – comprising three 35mm camera bodies – a 28mm, 35mm, 135mm and a 300mm lenses, a small flash, an exposure meter and film stock.

It was to be a long, hard walk, covering 15 miles on some days in rugged country, but a photographer's dream, walking on wind-blown ridges under beautiful mountains. The first red of the sun's rays hitting the highest peaks is something I will never forget; in a short time the whole range would be ablaze with the brilliant sunlight against a deep blue sky. The day would be spent walking, so I did most of my photography in the early morning and in the hour before dusk. It was at these times that I managed to get my studies of the local people. They were curious as we pitched our tents near the edge of their villages, the children being the most interested. though once we had made friends with them the barriers of shyness were broken down. My pictures show how well we got along together.

78. An old Victoria Cross winner and his wife posed for this picture high in a Himalayan village above the clouds (taken with a 135mm lens fitted with a three-times yellow filter).

79. Hands of the old V.C. winner gnarled by the rugged life in the Himalayas as he shows his Victoria Cross (also taken with a 135mm lens).

80. An ex-Gurkha sergeant poses against the background of Annapurna and Dhaulagiri (a picture taken with a 28mm lens through a three-times yellow filter, the aperture at f16 and the speed 1/60 second). This was an early-morning shot; as you can see, the strong hard shadows were causing problems and needed to be helped in the printing by shading the shadow detail.

81. These curious youngsters were photographed from inside my tent, looking out with a 135mm lens as they peered in at me. At this time I did not have a 75–150mm lens zoom but found the 135mm focal length adequate for the quick portrait before the subject had time to go shy and 'freeze'.

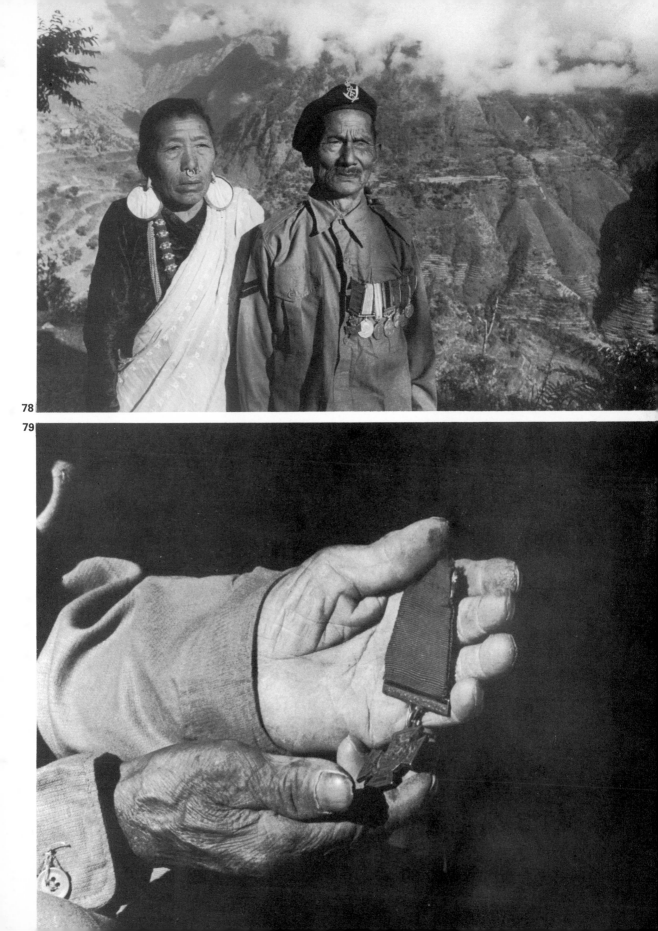

82–84. Loch Ness

These Loch Ness scenes were taken on a 35mm camera fitted with a 28mm lens and a three-times yellow filter. The shutter speed was 1/15 second with an aperture of f16. I chose not to use flash for these particular shots as I felt it would distract from the moody atmosphere of the loch.

85–96.   Northern Ireland

Belfast is only one hour's flying time from London. The contrast between the two cities is unbelievable. The television camera and news pictures have brought home to the rest of the world just how tragic the situation there is. For the photographers covering Northern Ireland it's a depressing and unwelcome assignment, but a subject that has to be reported and photographed. I think the still picture does this best; television supplements the visual impact with debates which diminish the pictorial dimension. The still picture says so much and needs little caption material. The still photographer must cover both sides of the troubles with no bias, record with his camera and let the pictures make their own comment.

A photographer working in Ireland would need the whole range of lenses from 28mm to 300mm, ideally having three cameras with these lenses attached. One lens I find extremely useful is the 75mm to 150mm zoom f4, very compact and light. While it's a good thing to let all sides know that you are a photographer, being over-equipped and bristling with too many cameras can result in confusion in certain situations. I show this selection of pictures purely from a photographic, not a political, point of view.

85. A British soldier shelters behind a street corner during a stone-throwing incident in Londonderry. The picture was taken on my 75mm to 150mm zoom lens set at 150mm, the speed 1/250 second at f5.6, the film Tri X.

86 & 87. Two pictures only seconds away, but which has more impact and sums up the events of that day in Belfast? Certain areas of the city were being burnt and bombed, forcing residents of both communities to flee their homes. The photograph with the lorry passing (No 87) is my choice; it did not matter about losing the firemen for they could have been attending a routine fire – the lorry gave a true impression of people fleeing with their possessions. Taken on a 35mm camera with 28mm lens at 1/250 second at f8, I made my point of focus halfway between building and foreground.

88. It is always a challenge to get something different. I repeated a photograph I first took during the troubles in Aden; this time it was the Ardoyne area of Belfast, looking from a British soldier's position through the telescopic sight of his rifle. The Ardoyne looked drab and miserable on this particular rainy day. The 35mm camera was fitted with a 28mm lens, the speed 1/15 second with aperture of f16.

89. The photograph of the soldier firing rubber bullets was taken in the late evening in Londonderry, the low light helping to make the smoke stand out and creating more atmosphere. For this photograph I used the zoom 75mm to 150mm lens set at 150mm with the aperture at f5.6, shutter speed 1/125 second. Extra development was given to the Tri X film.

90. Londonderry again, as a snatch squad of British soldiers grab a demonstrator. This was taken on 75mm–

150mm zoom at about 100mm, setting the speed at 1/125 second at f5.6. The strong back-lighting does little to help. With this type of exposure one must be careful when using through-camera metering, otherwise the shade areas will be very underexposed. Fortunately I do have the experience of what exposure to give without relying on meters.

91. A moment which required the photographer's discretion. That is why I chose to use a 135mm lens, careful not to be obtrusive. The scene is of children paying their last respects to their priest who had been killed in crossfire while attempting to help others in Belfast. Although indoors, the light was reasonably bright and allowed me to work without flash – which would have attracted the children's attention. The exposure was 1/60 second at f4 on Tri X film, pushing the film a little in development.

92. Ireland's countryside is renowned for its beauty; now even that is marred by political graffiti. This is a scene mid-way between Belfast and London-derry, taken on a 28mm lens fitted with a three-times yellow filter. The exposure was 1/60 second at f16 on Tri X film.

93. The Peace movement came to being through tragedy – Betty Williams and Maired Corrigan joined hands to symbolise its beginning. This picture is literally of the moment they did just that, at a mass demonstration in Belfast for their support after the death of some small children. Trying to get near them in the crowd was nearly impossible; this is where a motor drive is very handy. Being able to push the camera forward through the crowd, pointing it in the direction of the subjects, I got the photograph I might otherwise have missed. The Olympus camera (fitted with motor drive) was set for single exposures – the speed 1/250 second at f11 on Tri X film.

94 & 95. These two pictures of Northern Ireland were taken at Crossmaglen, the notorious stronghold of the I.R.A. I've always insisted that photographers should look for more than just the obvious; the Crossmaglen photos, I think, are a good example of spotting the off-beat picture. The small town looks peaceful enough in itself but it is in an area where many British soldiers have been killed or wounded from ambush. The outpost is the home of the British soldier who has to do a tour of duty there. It is reached and supplied by helicopter. I call it an outpost for that's all it is: high corrugated metal, sandbags and wire fences to ward off possible attack by rocket or small arms. It reminded me of an outpost one might have seen during the South African Boer War. For this reason I decided on the old-fashioned group picture, and titled it 'The Class of 75'. These men living in their confined area, only yards from the market square, lead an isolated life, becoming close friends, knowing each other's problems. Once outside the gates a sniper's bullet or a booby trap would give yet more heartache back home.

I sat them on their two armoured cars for the first

picture. It was some two weeks later that I photographed one of these armoured cars blown up by a
large bomb, and I'm sad to say that soldiers in the
group picture were killed and injured. These two
pictures are static; they are meant to be, recording a
very real part of the story of Northern Ireland.

The group picture was taken on a 28mm lens at
f11, with a shutter speed of 1/125 second. The
wrecked armoured car was taken on my zoom 75mm–
150mm lens at f5.6, also at 1/125 second on Tri X
film.

96. The portrait of a soldier on early-morning patrol
was taken at first light on a very dark, wet morning.
The shutter speed was 1/8 second at an aperture of
f3.5. The streaks on the right of the picture are caused
by the heavy rain and slow shutter speed. I gave this
film normal development, deliberately not uprating
the film – if I had done so the picture would have
been too contrasty and the tones would have clogged
the Tri X film.

85

4 Vietnam

One of the colour photographs I took when I was covering the Vietnam war (see Chapter 4, Assignments). Again, this was taken near the besieged town of Xuan Loc shortly before it was overrun by the North Vietnamese Communist forces, and shows wounded and blindfolded North Vietnamese prisoners; apart from the prisoner on the stretcher, who was too badly wounded to escape, they all had their hands bound behind their backs. There was an interesting light filtering down through the trees onto the bare brown earth below.

This photograph was taken with a 35mm camera using a 35mm lens; the speed was 1/60 second at f8, and the film was 64 A.S.A. Ektachrome.

5 Cyprus

I must admit there are the occasions when I get carried away, and on this occasion I thought I had a world scoop in the making. As the Turkish jet bombers and rockets hit Kyrenia, I was the only photographer there. There were bombs exploding to the right and left of me, but it was impossible to get the jet fighters into the same exposure. If I had had women and children running in the foreground this would have given the picture more news importance.

The photograph was taken on a 35mm lens on Ektachrome film.

6 Julie Ege

I took this photograph of Julie Ege on the uninhabited island in the Bahamas where the two of us spent a week making do without the trappings of modern civilisation – a good idea for a picture feature! (See the story and photographs in Chapter 6, Glamour and Fashion.)

I used a Hasselblad for this photograph with a 150mm lens. The speed was 1/125 second at f5.6 on 64 A.S.A. Ektachrome.

91

92

93

122

100–103. The Changing Face of Mr Niven

David Niven is the same charming man in real life as we see on the screen, yet when it comes to having his *own* character and personality photographed he's very shy. Like so many actors his shyness disappears behind the character he is portraying. Of these four shots the picture of David as himself (No 103) proved the most difficult, for we had an audience of film extras. Usually when photographing famous actors I try to avoid doing it in front of a crowd or disturbing what is happening naturally around them, for this attracts unwanted attention and makes the subject uneasy.

This series of pictures was taken over a period of seven weeks, yet in elapsed time no more than fifteen minutes was taken by the actual picture session. What saved a tremendous amount of time was knowing what I was after and I think Mr Niven appreciated this. Each time I visited the set he would pose for me within minutes of my arrival, which saved me many hours of waiting.

The pictures were taken on the set of the Walt Disney production of 'Candleshoe', using a 35mm camera fitted with an 85mm lens. The set itself was lit by floodlights corrected with daylight filters. This light filled in unwanted shadows for both monochrome and colour. I exposed the black and white Tri X at 1/250 second at f5.6, and the Ektachrome E4 at a speed of 1/125 second at f5.6, apart from No 102, taken in his dressing room at Pinewood Studios. This was taken on a 28mm lens at a speed of 1/60 second at f8, using bounced electronic flash at full power.

102

103

104 & 105. Memory Lane

Even a super star has a yen to go back down memory lane. James Stewart did just that when he visited his old war-time base in Norfolk. It was from here as a bomber pilot that he took off on war-time missions over Europe. Like all good stories it took several weeks to set up, but proved to be well worth the wait on the day.

I needed a certain amount of luck with the weather for the pictures I had in mind – any other condition would have ruined the whole operation. Mr Stewart's long association with Western films gave me my first idea (No 104) – a 'High Noon' effect as he strolled down the runway from which he once took off. Dramatic clouds and a lone silhouette figure did just that.

Another shot of the crumbling control tower made a perfect backdrop for the portrait (No 105).

The runway picture was taken from a low position to emphasise the figure against the sky – for the clouds, a three-times yellow filter was used. The 35mm camera was fitted with a 28mm lens, both pictures being exposed at a 1/250 second at f11.

106. American Horse Racing

I don't profess to be a sports photographer, but at times do get involved in sports features like this one at the races in Miami, Florida. It was one of many pictures in this series showing all aspects of the different approach of American racegoers to this sport. Whether it's Ascot or Florida the techniques are still the same.

For this picture, taken on a 300mm lens, the aperture at f8, I worked at a speed of 1/500 second. I panned the camera but did not want to create a blurred background. I panned to enable me to keep the subject in the centre of the picture, picking the riders up in my viewfinder for quite a distance before I pressed the button.

107. Friends

I suppose this would be considered a sport/animal picture. The sportsman is Henry Cotton, the world famous golfer, with Pacifico, his donkey and caddy. The picture was taken at Penina in Portugal. Mr Cotton, one of the greatest characters in golf, posed with Pacifico during a round of golf. The picture was used worldwide, and in most papers was lifted from the sports pages to the feature and news pages, where there is more space to give good picture layout. It was used as a major spread in the *Daily Express* as photonews, and given eight columns in space.

I chose a shaded area on the course for this particular shot and used a fill-in flash to clean up the mottled effect caused by the sun shining through the trees. My camera was fitted with a 35mm lens and the shot was at 1/60 second with an aperture of f11. I also shot this in colour – opening the aperture to f5.6 and f8, to get perfect results.

9 The Value of Light_____

Although the photographer and the artist in some ways work in parallel, a photographer would not claim to be a true artist, for he is mechanically aided, whereas an artist creates with brush, paint and canvas.

There are many artists I admire, particularly their skill in the way they bring a canvas to life, giving depth of focus and a life-like reality that I find photographically hard to follow. Battles of the past, showing men dying, the action pulled onto one large canvas, can be painted today. None I think re-creates these scenes better than the artist Terence Cuneo, whose studio I have visited on several occasions and where I have had the privilege of seeing him at work. I remember one commission he was working on, a mammoth-sized painting of a state banquet in London, which, even though far from the final stroke, was alive as if the event was then taking place. Another great artist I admire tremendously is the American Norman Rockwell, whose inimitable work decorated the front of the *Saturday Evening Post* for many years, displaying with uncanny reality the American way of life. He recorded the seasons, the Christmas period with holly and Christmas trees – all aspects of American (particularly small-town American) life to grace the front of the *Post*. The depth and sharpness of detail is something the camera could never truly record as do Cuneo and Rockwell in their paintings; an artist can move detail seen at another time into his present work, photographers can only photograph what is there at the moment. Nevertheless, a parallel we do have: we both create pictures with landscape, people and machinery.

Here is one thing a photographic journalist should consider – will he take 'straight' pictures of the person or event as it happens, will he distort them with a wide-angled lens, or will he mis-use the light and misrepresent the mood or atmosphere of the time or even of the year of taking that picture. Where the artist is in a privileged position and can paint our yesterday, our present or future as he sees it, one can never be quite sure if what he portrays is as it was. Did it really happen and look just quite like that? On the other hand the photographer can capture events exactly as they happened, to be looked at in years to come and record a true representation of events in time. For instance, the assassination of President Kennedy – a true moment of time caught with the camera.

A second parallel with the artist is light – something many photographers take for granted, unlike the artist who sees hidden pictures in each pool of light reaching a corner of a room or forest. The photographer must take advantage of the great strides that have been made chemically and mechanically in photography. Fast films, electronic flashes with built-in sensors to measure precisely the available light, perfect through-lens metering built into the cameras, the motor drive – they are all useless unless we exploit light to the full. The simple electronic flash is so often used without thinking. There is probably little one can do on a news story where it is as dark as the Black Hole of Calcutta, except perhaps to ensure that you or the light are well placed and that the latter is not reflected back into the camera by glass or a mirror, or then again to find later that you have fixed the flash in too low a position that only exaggerates dark shadows behind. Beginner's stuff, maybe, but the mistakes are made by so many. The photographer has an advantage in his electronic flash, for it can complement the natural light available. The bounced flash picture became popular in the late 1950s when the electronic flash took over from the bulb and other primitive equipment. During the flash bulb period photographers would go to great trouble with extension flashes and yards of cable to produce pictures, and it cannot be denied that some of their results were superb. Today, unfortunately, we've been made lazy with the small transistorised flash units, and many rely on the bounced or direct flash for their work. At times I think we miss the opportunities that natural light affords, not utilising it to advantage with just a little thought and care taken to improve the picture.

When working on your own on feature stories, try using two or three flashes with small 'slave' units to fire these away from the camera. This can give a pleasing light if hidden behind an object, throwing the subject clear from possible darkness and giving highlighting on the hair or a sparkle which with one direct flash would have been absent. Using more than one flash can eliminate shadows and that flatness resulting from straight bounced light. I've mentioned the use of flash outdoors, using filters and bouncing it into umbrellas. This is all very simple; it only needs a little extra effort and familiarity with the equipment, and you will gradually achieve perfection. Fortunately the sophisticated metering in cameras can't produce the results of a professional photographer's personal experience. Where there is tricky light, or where you need to balance light evenly, it is that personal know-how that gives you the best results. Bounced flash used with natural indoor lighting can be very effective, provided the light is balanced to avoid over-bouncing which would result in the loss of the natural-light effect. The really successful bounced light requires more powerful electronic flash units, especially in large high areas. When combining natural light and bounced flash, I find it better to rely on one's own evaluation of the light – what is the strength of the metered natural light? Taking that into account, I work with full or half-power electronic flash. At times my shutter speed could be as low as 1/8 second with an aperture of f8. I've chosen this aperture and speed to give more depth of focus in my photograph without losing the natural light. If I had worked at 1/30 or 1/60 second, the bounced light would have outweighed the natural light and I would then have lost the atmosphere that I was after.

One story I covered not long ago, using this method, was of Mohammed Ali at home in Chicago (photos 108–9). It was one of those stories that came out of the blue and I was very ill-prepared for this sort of personal feature – I had been travelling for three weeks on more newsy stories. Usually, for a feature story at someone's home, I would use several flashes with umbrellas. Instead, I had my two small units that I usually carry in my camera bag, and they were not the ideal equipment for this. I was photographing a high-powered personality in his home – another added problem. This was an exclusive story – no photographer had ever got into King Ali's castle! – and I could not afford to fail, and this assignment was made more difficult by the fact that I was unable to see any of the interior of the house beforehand. As each door opened, a different photographic situation arose. Ali himself gave me a lightning tour. He was courteous and charming but, as in the ring, he moved swiftly, posing for me from kitchen to bathroom. It was all over in thirty minutes, the time I would normally take to set up my cameras on one of these features.

I decided from the start to keep the photography simple, allowing myself two cameras, one loaded with colour and the other black and white, a flash on each. Immediately I realised that the small flash units I carried would not have the power to bounce with colour, so I set the dial for the correct A.S.A. speed on the colour camera as required, and kept the flash attached to the camera. For these pictures I worked at speeds of 1/8 and 1/15 second with an aperture of f5.6, letting the sensor read off the correct flash exposure. The slow shutter speed was to try and pick up just that bit of natural light; even though it was Tungsten light I was not bothered about colour balance. I was trying to give just that something more than a straightforward flash picture.

For the black and white I could just get away with bouncing. My aperture was around f4 and I also used a speed of 1/8 and 1/15 second. The flash was set at full power, working on manual.

The story itself is what I would call an 'in and out' story – in and out in more ways than one, which all went to help build up my adrenalin. I was in sunny Los Angeles one moment when the opportunity came up to photograph Ali. I flew overnight to Chicago. Arriving in a blizzard in the early morning, I waited till five o'clock in the evening to photograph the great Mohammed Ali, and that same evening caught a flight back to London.

When using flash, things can go wrong in the excitement of the moment – incorrect synchronisation settings, then total disaster. Even today flashes seem temperamental at times, and there is always the possibility that one might misjudge the available light. Then I wonder, should I have worked at 1/60 second and done everything by the book and ignored trying to bounce the flash for black and white, or used that little bit of natural light with the colour? Don't experiment with an important story, but once you find your level of ability, don't be afraid to use it. That is just what I was doing on this assignment, even though on that flight to London I was nervous about the exposure and the quality of lighting I had actually got on my pictures. In the end, all these misgivings were groundless; when I saw the final results, I was well pleased with the photographs. They were not of the optimum quality, but what I had shot in those thirty minutes was more than adequate and they caused great interest in many magazines and newspapers. If I had taken longer with the photography or had complicated matters with umbrellas, other lights and the like, I think I would have not got the amount of material I did. Ali was a man who had very little time; he might have left me in the hallway still struggling to work out different readings and the other things you like to do beforehand, so on balance it was fortunate that I had only those two small flash units!

If there is a choice between using natural light and flash I usually go for the natural light. Creating 'natural' light in the studio and simulating its special quality is made easy by the powerful strobe lighting of today, but working on location is another thing. If you create extra light you must do so for a good reason – like cleaning up shadows. You can spend a great deal of time, money and energy in creating good lighting. It requires a lot of know-how to appreciate particular lighting requirements. I had the good fortune to be invited onto the set of a film recently being made in Austria, 'The Prisoner of Zenda', starring Peter Sellers and his wife Lynn Frederick, to take some photographs of the wedding scene of the King of Zenda – a scene of great splendour set in a cathedral on the outskirts of Vienna (see photos 110–11). On film sets the lighting cameraman does a tremendous job and this was probably one of the most clever lighting scenes I have ever seen. It was made difficult primarily by the shape of the cathedral and the need to conceal the cables and all the other trappings of the setting up of the lighting of a film scene. The light and the atmosphere were all there, and fortunately on such occasions the still photograph does capture these effectively. It reminded me of the time I photographed Princess Margaret's wedding inside Westminster Abbey. The lighting on that occasion also was very effective – trying to light scenes like these with flash or strobe lighting would have been almost impossible. I required no flashes of any kind for these pictures; indeed, if I had attempted to use a flash it might have detracted from the atmosphere created there. I was able to work at a speed of 1/125 second at f5.6 on colour, 1/250 second with the same aperture on black and white.

On another occasion, an international indoor cycle meeting at Wembley Empire Pool, with floodlights providing very good lighting, I decided to put the flash on my camera (photos 112–13). Other photographers were working with available light only, but for my pictures I decided to use three flashlights to give more impact for a different effect; I also wanted to employ the flash in conjunction with the motor drive. I used the three flashes to cast more shadows, to give a different lighting from that which one flash would have given, and at the same time to stop that moment of time that it takes for a bike to move maybe half a yard – to freeze the moment of strain on the cyclist's face. If I had shot with available light I would have panned my camera but would not have got the depth of focus or the crispness you get with an aperture of f11 using the flash. The shadow detail would also have gone; there would not have been that clarity about the whole photograph.

Many photographers talk about using light, painting with light, but in photography in general this can be done a little too much – the camera is not designed to paint with. Of course, I've panned my camera to make movement in the background and to freeze the object moving through the air but it has been done for a reason. For the picture of Eddie Kidd, the stunt rider (photos 114–16), I panned the camera, deliberately working at a slow shutter speed at 1/30 second with an aperture of f11 to cut down the amount of light, otherwise the picture would have been overexposed. The reason for the slow speed was to blur the background and give the effect of speed. Another time I was working with some soldiers of the S.A.S. (photo 117). Now this is a very tightly knit security unit and I was not allowed to identify or show their faces. There were several ways I could do this – either to block their faces out or try to create a blurred image, at the same time trying to capture on film some of the intrigue and excitement of what the S.A.S. do, being an élite force of under-cover soldiers. Here again I used a very slow speed, 1/8 second stopped right down to f16. It was on a very bad day – very poorly lit – and the shot I got was pleasing and effective. But this is an example of using light properly; whether it's flash or daylight, you use it for an effect.

As with the overuse of the wide-angled lens, I also don't particularly like the bending of light to unrecognisable proportions. A photograph is something that somebody can recognise tomorrow and realise what it was exactly like at the moment of taking, without having to wonder what on earth they are looking at. Light is the most important thing in photography; to distort it, to misuse it, is a photographic crime. By all means diffuse it, by all means blur it to an extent. You can create impact or moodiness with or without flash, but don't over-distort it. This sort of misuse is not my kind of photography and it is not picture-journalism. To hark back to what I said at the beginning of the chapter, our job is to capture the mood, the atmosphere, even on occasion to introduce in the picture rather more mood than there actually was, but don't distort it beyond recognition.

While on the subject of light I ought to mention the practice of 'up-rating' films – something I avoid if possible, though on occasions I've pushed black and white over two stops when the light was extremely poor. Once was while taking pictures from a helicopter over the North Sea of some disaster in atrocious weather as the last light of a wintry day was fading; another time was on a dawn patrol in Northern Ireland I had no choice but to push. Pushing your film I would only recommend as a last resort. Increased grain can make a picture look a little bit special but it has to be of the right subject. I don't think it very fashionable to produce grainy pictures that break up detail. Furthermore, they don't help to make a quality reproduction in a newspaper or magazine. In my view, you can get away with pushing colour a little bit more than monochrome. I do this even when using the new Ektachrome E6, which can be pushed one or two stops. I've also found it very handy to have both colour and black and white rated at the same A.S.A. of 400. Colour does hold the detail that much more; contrast does possibly increase a little and there is a small amount of colour change, though nothing to worry about.

If you do uprate your films, remember to mark these when putting them in for processing, especially colour film, because it is in the first developer that the increased time of development is given. The black and white can, if necessary, be intensified, but with colour it's undesirable to start fiddling about after missing the extra time needed in development. A colour transparency can be improved when duplicated, of course, but you will obviously lose a certain amount of quality and detail. It's only been in recent months that the very fast colour film has come onto the market. I feel that, with available light and with modern electronic flashes, this new film has opened up a completely new era in photography. Things are changing so rapidly now that what was impossible only a few years ago is today easily achieved by a photographer capable of using these strides forward in photography to his advantage. I believe these will bring a new look to photography as did the original 35mm cameras – they were so different from the old photographs taken on half-plate cameras of years ago. With the synchronisation of Compur shutters to a five-hundredth of a second and the introduction of the electronic flash firing at a ten-thousandth of a second, it has enabled us to look at life frozen for ever. It introduced a new style of photography, yet the old picture of a group, taken at an exposure of some 30 seconds, is still as interesting as a photograph of a bullet caught in mid-action as it smashes a glass. I wonder if we will use the new-found fast colour film to create beautiful quality combined with a large format camera aided by the sophisticated electronic flash. Will these give us the same success in picture-journalism as it did our colleagues of years ago, whose pictures are now being pulled from the archives and reprinted in many books and magazines for our pleasure and enjoyment?

108 & 109. At Home With Mohammed Ali

These pictures were taken by bounced flash. On this story I worked with shutter speeds of 1/8 second and 1/15 second using black and white and colour film. The reason for this slow exposure was to allow for a certain amount of natural light to be picked up adding to the atmosphere. I used a stop of f5.6 to give some depth of focus.

No 108 was taken on a 35mm camera fitted with a 28mm lens. The close-up of Mohammed Ali and daughter (No 109) was taken at f8. Tri X film was used in both pictures.

109

110 & 111. Royal Wedding

Wedding of the King of Zenda, played by Peter Sellers, to the princess, played by his real-life wife Lynn Frederick, in the film 'The Prisoner of Zenda'.

    This is one instance where having three camera bodies was essential. For scenes where many actors and extras are involved, the Director likes to move quickly. For this scene I was shooting black and white and colour. The wide angle shot (No 110) was taken on a 28mm lens and the close-up (No 111) on my zoom 150mm lens, using a 85mm on the colour camera, quickly changing the 28mm lens on to the colour camera to give me full coverage both in full close-up and wide angle in monochrome and colour. Fortunately Mr Sellers is very considerate to the photographer; being a very good still photographer himself he understood my requirements, making sure I had my picture safely in the bag before moving.

The light was of very good quality and allowed a reasonable fast shutter speed of 1/250 second at f5.6 on black and white, and 1/125 with the same aperture in colour.

114–116. Eddie Kidd

Eddie Kidd, Britain's answer to America's Evil Knievel. This sequence was taken on an Olympus fitted with a motor drive as Eddie was practising for a world-record attempt. Normally the motor drive would have given me an extra couple of exposures if I had been using a faster shutter speed, but I wanted to pan the camera to create the impression of speed and still retain sharpness, so I selected a speed of 1/30 second. I used an aperture of f11 to ensure the correct exposure on Tri X film, but not for depth of focus. I find working much faster than 1/30 second is inclined to hold the background too sharp, thus losing the effect of speed. In fact on some occasions I have worked as slow as 1/8 second (for the S.A.S. picture, No 117) to give more dramatic effect, though no picture subject should be unrecognisable because of blur. The lens was 85mm.

117. S.A.S. in Training

This picture of members of the Special Air Services
is blurred to make the subjects unrecognisable for
security reasons – and again to give the picture some
of the atmosphere which these undercover men work
in. The exposure was at 1/8 second. As they rushed
past me, panning the camera helped to freeze the
most important part of the picture, even though their
features are unrecognisable. But at the same time you
can still see the urgency of their work. The guns that
are the main tools of their trade have hardly been
affected by the movement in the rest of the picture.

The 35mm camera was fitted with a 28mm lens;
aperture was f16 on Tri X film.

118–121. The Green March

The 'Green March' in Morocco demanded much physical and mental determination and a lot of luck. The story took place in a remote part of the Spanish Sahara, which meant driving for many hours and miles through a sandstorm, arguing with Government officials and other photographers, the whole thing made more difficult as none spoke English. My luck came when I was able to get myself and my films back to London, beating the opposition, which enabled us to market our original material to many countries exclusively.

Having made my way eventually to the area where the march took place, I was faced with dust and sand blown by a strong wind – the curse of any photographer. Although the sun could not be seen, it was still strong enough to create a very uninteresting light. Here again I was careful not to overexpose, otherwise the negatives would have been dense and grainy and hard to print. On all the lenses I used a u.v. filter and, using them as required from 28mm to 300mm, the average exposure was at 1/500 second at f8. The colour seemed moreeffective than black and white in these conditions – in the white haziness colours looked more vivid. I was exposing the Ektachrome 160 A.S.A. high speed at 1/250 second at f8.

No 118 is of a queue for water in a dust storm, Nos 119 & 120 are of the march in progress, in which some 350,000 people took part, and No 121 is of myself on the march.

10 Cameras and Lenses

There is no need to assemble great quantities of equipment, but I would like to stress that what you do acquire should be of good quality. Another point that should have some influence on your decision when purchasing your equipment is the situation regarding service and repairs (yes, cameras do go wrong, and in photo-journalism we push them to their limits). I hear of people waiting months for the simplest of repairs; for a photographer who has taken my advice and has only the minimum amount of equipment this can be difficult, especially when it is a camera body that has failed. I personally like to know that I have three camera bodies, all in very good working order, in my camera bag. If a lens goes out of action I can usually get around this by making do with a different focal length.

The mechanics of a camera body do not need explaining; just follow the instruction manual. It is the lens that one really has to understand, so I give my own interpretation of lenses, how I use them to their best advantage, and how I visualise what each lens can do.

Most photographic equipment is only as good as the photographer. Of course, the lens is the exception; it is something special to the photographer when he really understands it and uses it with feeling. He must know exactly how much 'bite' it has (by this I mean quality and sharpness), when to give it a bit of stop (aperture) and how much depth he is getting in the photograph. A really good lens makes a tremendous difference to quality.

The lens I consider my normal one is the 28mm f2 wide-angled lens; it's approximately what I see with my eyes photographically without distortion. I know the 50mm lens is normally considered to show what the human eye discerns in colour and shape, but I feel that for my style of photography the 28mm lens does it better. If I used a wider-angled lens I would not be able to control unnecessary distortion, something I always try and eliminate.

The 28mm lens gives me control. The 28mm lens gives me the depth I need in the type of photograph I take, incorporating atmosphere as well. It is also good for photographing people. For semi-close-up portraits I usually have my subject just under two yards from the camera; I can still get the background reasonably sharp using an aperture of f8, while stopping down to an aperture of f16 would give me overall sharpness. I focus on the face and rely on the stop to pull in what background sharpness is needed.

When photographing people with a 28mm I keep the lens level with the centre of the subject (this too helps cut out distortion), also being careful not to get the subject too small. When photographing events keep the main subject bold; because of the 28mm's focal length things are that much sharper. Watch out for buildings, poles and the like which might detract from the subject. Try to create a pleasant true-to-life picture with a natural atmosphere.

Some photographers prefer a 35mm lens for general use; I used one for many years together with a 21mm wide-angled lens but finally decided to adopt the 28mm in preference to these two lenses. I also shoot landscape pictures with the 28mm lens – it captures the panorama without losing any of the detail needed in good landscape photography. Again, the wide aperture allows one to work even at night by street lighting, which would normally require a tripod. Using the through-the-lens metering system and holding the camera still, I can take my picture with as little fuss as possible.

Now we come to the 50mm lens, a lens I rarely use. It is very good for portraits when you do not require background with atmosphere. It is also useful for working in bad light by virtue of its wide aperture, though for me it has limited general use, especially in confined spaces; even so, it is probably very popular with many photographers.

A lens I use frequently is the 75mm to 150mm zoom f4, a good all-round lens giving a quick selection of different focal lengths. It does not have the bite of the other lenses. Like all zooms it lacks that little edge of sharpness, though only fractionally, and many would not even notice on the print. It is a very good lens for news assignments, very compact and light; even when used with a flash at its maximum focal length of 150mm it has proved very successful. Its shortest focal length of 75mm approximates to the normal standard 50mm lens; I would prefer a little wider aperture than the f4, but you can't have everything!

Because of the zoom's relative slowness at f4 aperture I also carry an 85mm f2. What a good lens this is! The quality is really outstanding; even at f2 the point of focus is critically sharp. This lens is good for very close-up portraits where just a little or no background is required. It is obviously good for working in poor lighting conditions; in fact, in these circumstances it produces very moody pictures. It is an in-between lens, small, yet powerful. One can stand back in a crowd and get pictures of people with plenty of atmosphere and not be noticed. I like to use it with colour because of its wide aperture.

My next lens up from the zoom is a 300mm f4.5, but I have a good two-times tele-converter that fits all my lenses, so I am well covered between 175mm and 300mm. The 300mm lens is very sharp; it is a very important lens in the telephoto range and is the longest I carry. It has a reasonably wide aperture, is light in weight and good in quality. I use this lens for most assignment photographs, including fashions and even portraits. It is ideal for trouble spots, enabling you to pick off incidents that don't happen under your feet. You are inclined to use it more on the big international stories where photographers are kept at a distance, as well as for Royal tours or close-up pictures of the Royal Family. When working with this lens I prefer to use a motor drive or motor wind, avoiding the need to wind on the film by hand, and this enables one to concentrate on holding the camera still. I like the foreshortening effect the 300mm gives with its out-of-focus background when not using too much stop; it is ideal for sports photography, car racing and the like. The tele-converter gives me a facility equal to a 600mm lens, though I lose two stops and only get an aperture of f8, but with today's fast colour film equal to monochrome it causes no problems. This gives me a very powerful telephoto lens without the weight problem normally associated with this equipment. To carry the usual 600mm would be impossible on the type of assignment that I am required to do as part of the day's work.

Photographers in journalism choose their equipment to suit their jobs. The crime photographer carries the least of any photographer, usually one small camera that fits comfortably into a jacket or raincoat pocket, with a small electronic flash. He can go about his job unrecognised and wait until the opportunity arises to take his photograph. At the other end of the scale is the sports photographer, who requires the most equipment of all, using very long lenses of 1000mm or more to enable him to capture a certain picture. The motor drive is a must for the sports photographer, who can be excused for keeping his finger on the button when working – he must get that one sharp picture in case some world record is being broken.

Most cameras have through-the-lens metering systems. They are very reliable but problems do occur, especially in difficult lighting. I use the meters on my cameras and find them accurate provided I watch what light they are reading. It is popular practice for photographers to have separate exposure meters; I use one myself – a Weston – which, used in conjunction with the camera's own meter, ensures perfect exposures. When taking a picture of a subject in the shade when it cannot be moved and where the background is brilliantly lit, I take my exposure reading on the subject and sometimes augment this by pointing the camera into a similarly shaded area. I always use the Weston meter with the Invercone; with this I take readings from a similar light position to that of the subject, pointing the Invercone directly towards the camera. Using the Invercone in this way gives me consistently good exposures.

Before moving on to another part of photography, I feel I should go into the subject of meters and meter reading with flash. In the studio I use a special electronic flash exposure meter. If I'm mixing daylight and flash together, the flash is sometimes mounted on a stand some five to seven yards away. I look to see how the flash lights the subject under the eyes or under the chin. When I know my flash will not kill the daylight but give just enough light to illuminate the shadow, then I know the exposure is about correct. However, when taking the easy way at times, I try to look for a shaded bright area where no flash fill-in is required, and then I will just work straight from the meters on the camera, providing there is no harsh back-light coming through that might give a false reading.

Another thing to be careful about when photographing in daylight with flashlight is a double image. If movement is required then it is obviously better to use a Compur (between-lens) shutter, which facilitates synchronisation with electronic flash, at a faster shutter speed – as much as 1/500 second. The focal plane 35mm camera unfortunately does give problems because one is limited to 1/60 or 1/125 second with electronic flash. I try not to get too clever with daylight flash. If I'm shooting movement I seldom attempt to mix too much flash with daylight unless I'm trying for an effect. If I need movement and want more light on the subject without using flash then I try photographing slightly against the light, using reflector boards to clean up the shadows.

Small flashlights today are very sophisticated little pieces of equipment, most having their own light sensors which do the thinking for you on exposures for flashlight photography. The majority are reasonably priced and are perhaps the best value of all photographic equipment. The smaller electronic flashes, having less battery power, take longer in build-up time of course. The photographer who requires a faster recycling time should go in for the larger (and more expensive) flash equipment, some of which will enable him to work with a motor drive or motor wind without pausing. For a news photographer this is vital – an important person can rush from a door and into a car, trying to hide his face – and getting off five or six exposures gives you a better chance of getting a facial picture than you would if you only managed to get one shot off with inadequate equipment.

The majority of photographers are now using the 35mm format. Most of those specialising in fashion use the $2\frac{1}{4}$ square format and, of course, there are some photo-journalists who still use the Rolleiflex for everyday use in preference to the 35mm. The larger format cameras are rarely used today, except for architectural and other specialised purposes. Rolleiflex and Hasselblad are the most popular cameras in the $2\frac{1}{4}$ square range; a photographer who uses these is usually very quality conscious, and I admit that the quality is a little better than 35mm. It is the compactness of the 35mm that we need for the majority of our work – this makes the final decision when equipping ourselves. Over the years I have changed the make of my equipment several times, but not the format size; this was simply due to wear and tear and having equipment stolen.

In the last ten years equipment has improved dramatically, not that I think the lens standard has improved a great deal. The actual mechanical workings have improved so, in taking advantage of these new techniques, I have changed my equipment.

Since starting to use 35mm in 1957, however, my choice of different focal length lenses and the number of camera bodies that I now carry on assignments remains more or less the same, and at this stage in my life I see no reason why I should change.

Photographers have the terrible habit of becoming collectors of cameras. Every time a new bit of equipment appears on the market, they are like boys seeing a new toy – they want it. Well, I don't think one needs to worry too much about assembling great quantities of equipment providing the equipment you get is practical and reliable and you feel comfortable with it. Most good makes of camera are basically the same, some heavier, some lighter. I go for the lighter type of camera. Today, cameras and lenses within a given price range are very similar in quality; some may have the edge on others but on the whole they are pretty reliable in their end results. Be careful not to become frightened to use your equipment; by this I mean to scratch it, or knock it, or get it covered in dust. If you are a photo-journalist on assignments you will work under conditions that can be hot and dusty one day, with torrential rain the next. Your camera must be rugged enough to go through these and remain operational. I find that by not pampering my equipment it seems to remain stronger and lasts that much longer, giving the impression that it's more rugged. However, camera manufacturers might think differently. Maybe other photographers like to take more care, but for me the equipment must be used to the maximum and give reliability at all times. Nevertheless, before I put it all away at night I clean it thoroughly.

Assignments are costly and excuses are not acceptable in my book. The photographer is the one responsible for producing, so keep your gear if not tidy then compact. Don't get overcomplicated. If you find the job at hand is too difficult, handle it in the way you are best able to produce your best results. Never experiment with your photography while on an assignment; by all means do so in your spare time, but not at the cost of ruining or missing pictures when working. Make sure you can operate your equipment with confidence at all times. You achieve this while playing with unloaded cameras, changing films quickly, unloading and reloading.

Single-lens reflex cameras can give certain photographers with eye trouble focussing problems. I have this trouble and there are several small correction lenses that will fit to the back of your camera to adapt your eyes to the rest of the focussing system. I have met several of my colleagues who have gone on for years with this trouble; they say they can't understand why they are unable to get their photographs sharp! Simply purchasing this little lens, at a very low cost, has solved this problem for them.

122. Hunted

I found Ronald Biggs living a lonely existence, except for the company of his young son, in a run-down Portuguese fishing village 50 miles south of Rio de Janeiro – a man desperately wanting to return to England but unable to do so as he is wanted by Scotland Yard for his part in the Great Train Robbery. Brazil is his last and only place of refuge. After I arrived in the capital it was easy enough to contact Biggs on the telephone and fix my interview for a fee of $50.

These pictures were taken on the 75mm–150mm zoom lens and exposed at 1/250 second at f4 on black and white, and 1/125 second at f4 on colour. The zoom lens was ideal for all the photography. It gave some of the atmosphere of his existence without calling for any posing that was too unnatural, and at the same time was fine for the portrait of Biggs and his son Mike.

123. Leila Khaled

Leila Khaled took part in the attempted hijacking of an Israeli airliner in 1971. She posed for me with her grandfather in a Palestinian refugee camp on the outskirts of Beirut. Permission for the photograph took a considerable time setting up. First of all I had to be cleared by the Palestinian Intelligence; for this I waited two weeks in Beirut, never certain if I would be finally granted the opportunity to take photographs of her. When I was eventually given the go-ahead, Leila was charming and courteous during the session, although at times her armed bodyguards made me feel a little uneasy.

The picture was taken on a 28mm lens at f11, with a shutter speed of 1/125 second on Tri X film.

124. Guildford Bombing

The Guildford pub bombing was a major news story that happened only a few minutes' drive from my home late on a Saturday evening. There were two explosions several minutes apart which killed seven people; the man in the photograph, though badly injured, was one of the luckier ones.

But, to the details of the photograph. Having an early tip about the first blast I was arriving on the scene just as the second had gone off. After fixing a flash frantically to my camera I started taking pictures, but found the flash was not firing (later I found that the camera lead was faulty). This left me one alternative, and that was to stop the aperture down to f16 and work with open flash at full power – not the most efficient way to cover a story, but it did get me results. Admittedly, the failure rate was high; of approximately eighteen exposures only five came out. This photograph was used on the front page of the final edition of the *Sunday Mirror* and splashed in all the Monday morning daily papers.

The 35mm camera was fitted with a 28mm lens, the film Kodak Tri X.

125

126

125. Ian Smith

Ian Smith photographed at a Press conference in Salisbury. The picture was taken with strong television lights on a 300mm lens at an aperture of f8 with shutter speed at 1/60 second.

A long lens can be effective for portraits, especially at Press conferences where it is not always possible to get close enough to your subject. It was quite comfortable working like this, not having to strain into some awkward position as you might have to when working close-up with a different focal length lens. I was sitting in a chair with the camera on a mono-pod; the print is nearly the full frame of the negative. Another yard closer and it would have been impossible to focus down to get Mr Smith clear and sharp. I needed the aperture of f8 to achieve some depth of focus; not too much, but just enough to make him stand out from a confused background.

The film was Tri X. I also shot this in colour using Tungsten film. Something one should watch when photographing in colour by floodlights – find out what the real light source is. Is it daylight or artificial?

126. Rhodesian Tragedy

This picture was taken at the funeral of Mrs Helen Taylor and her daughter Sue, killed by a terrorist ambush. Her husband and son stand alone at the graveside in Chipinga.

It was a difficult picture to take – I wanted to avoid intruding on this moment of grief – but it sums up the tragic situation that exists in Rhodesia. Usually it's the women who seem to weep on such occasions, but now Mr Taylor and his son suffer the ultimate grief.

I photographed this scene on a 300mm lens, sheltering behind some bushes. I took three exposures. It is not a 'sneak' picture. I stood behind the bush to avoid intrusion on their grief and, having taken it, withdrew quietly.

Taken at 1/500 second at f5.6 on Tri X film.

127. A Delicate Situation

This photograph of Prince Charles attending the funeral of President Kenyatta of Kenya led off the main news stories in the world press, not because of the Royal attendance but because of a near Royal confrontation between Prince Charles and President (as he was then) Amin of Uganda, whose presence caused embarrassment to the more respectable nations. The newspapers claimed that Prince Charles snubbed President Amin by turning his back, and this story overshadowed the funeral itself. Photographically, this incident wasn't observed; all we could get was a shot of President Amin separated by the other African Heads of State. The photograph captures Prince Charles taking the odd sly glance at Amin.

It was taken on a 300mm lens foreshortening the whole picture (closing up the figures). The distance was about 20 yards, at an aperture of f8 and a speed of 1/125 second on Tri X film, using a motor drive set on single exposure on a 35mm camera.

11 A Brief Look at the Darkroom; Step by Step

I can't over-emphasise the importance of darkroom experience; those starting in the profession at a young age will gain it in time, but the established photographer should know darkroom working inside out.

I offer these few simple tips on very basic ground rules to the fringe photo-journalist; by this I mean those who may try their hand at our profession when the opportunity presents itself. Most writers I know today carry automatic cameras – they may be covering some exclusive event where no photographers are present – and they sometimes seek my advice on improving their photography. I'm also asked by business men, air stewards and the like: 'How can I take good pictures?' They often see things of interest during their travels, and unfortunately their pictures are ruined by ignorance during processing.

There are many good books on darkroom working. Photographic printing is an art in itself, so I will confine myself to basic photography.

Cameras are made by engineers; films and photographic chemicals are produced by chemists. The marriage of the two, through the photographer, takes place in the darkroom, whether in black and white or colour. Let us take black and white to begin with, for we must understand that first. A film exposed and ready for developing introduces our first rule, a rule that you should apply in all your darkroom working: strive for quality. Providing the film has been exposed by a competent photographer, there is no reason why first-class prints should not be completed well within an hour.

There may be times when you will be required to produce prints in 15 to 30 minutes and still retain quality. There could be other rare occasions when you will be working under extreme and urgent conditions to process wire-prints for transmitting back to newspaper offices. But this should cause no difficulty to the properly trained operator.

Correct film developing is vital, for it is here that the most important step is taken; simple mistakes in the developing of an assignment of mine could cost thousands of pounds and end in complete disaster. It is here that you determine the quality; always aim for a good negative. I work with high-speed film, as do most of us who cover news events, and where possible (and that is nearly always) I use a fine grain developer to give me the best possible negative.

Developing film is in itself very easy; after a month of training you should know what first-class negatives are and be able to produce them. The mixing of chemicals is of the utmost importance, for wrong mixing can result in crystallisation. If not done properly it can also cause marks that cannot be removed from the film's emulsion.

The developer must be at the right temperature; too cold and it won't develop fully, too hot and you will coarsen the grain and produce a 'thick' negative which reduces definition and makes printing a tiresome task. If the developer is fresh and too hot this will also double the grain size, which will ruin the definition.

I prefer to use developer that is about a week old; it seems to mature like good wine. My preferred developer is Kodak D76, which gives an average development time of about ten minutes, producing a good standard negative from a normally exposed film.

Of course photographers work in varied and difficult conditions around the world. Light can often be in short supply, or it can be too glaring with heavy shadows. For this reason we never change the developer until it is exhausted, which enables the darkroom staff to monitor their developing standard at a temperature of approximately 70°F (21°C). By using this method you know exactly the type of negative to expect. You can always gauge the developer's strength and what it will do.

If a photographer has underexposed, we simply give the extra development time that is required; if the film is overexposed, then we give it a minute or two less than normal. As the developer gets older, we increase development times on all types of films to the time we know is required. When the developer is a month old and the development time reaches about 14 minutes, the developer is nearing exhaustion; it has processed a certain number of films and so we change it, at the same time changing the fixing bath to maintain uniformity in our film processing.

Another simple thing to remember in these early stages when handling undeveloped films is to keep your fingers off the emulsion before and after putting films into developer. Before the developed film is dry and safely in the negative bag it is very vulnerable to scratches or marking. Believe me, it always seems to happen on the most important negative, so it is vital that the film is handled with care.

In our film developing darkroom we have three tanks within one thermostatically-controlled unit, for developer, fixer and water. As I said before, it is important that the developer be kept at a constant temperature. The water is there for one reason only, for emergency. We use spirals in our darkroom and sometimes a film does get stuck when loading. If this happens we immerse both spiral and film in the water and then wind on normally. Immersion then enables the film to be fed into the spiral freely. Remember, if you do immerse make sure the film is not caught up, or it will stick together once it gets wet.

The fixer is a much hardier chemical than the developer. If you get fixer mixed into the developer it becomes useless. On the other hand, developer does not destroy the fixer. It will, of course, dilute it over a period of time and possibly contaminate it, but this can be rectified with a topping-up of the fixer with concentrated liquid. Also, you must remember to mix enough hardener with your fixer to prevent the film emulsion becoming too soft and susceptible to scratching and marking. I use a rapid fixer, which gives me a fixing time for my film of two to three minutes. Fixing makes the developed emulsion permanent and incapable of being changed by exposure to light. Many people remove their film from the fixer looking milky – but it needs to be put back for extra fixing.

You must adopt systematic working in the darkroom, because working in the dark with film spirals or cassettes in a jumble can be disastrous. I have known it happen when developing several films simultaneously for one to be left out of the developer in the spirals that are on the worktop – there is no need for me to make any comment on this! What I suggest is that before you turn the white light out to start your film processing you check that you have a

can opener, which is handy for taking the tops off the 35mm cassettes easily; check that you have a pair of scissors for trimming the ends of the film (cutting these square will enable the film to go into spirals more easily); check that you have a towel; and check that you have enough spirals to take the number of films to be developed.

It is best to work from one side to the other of your work bench. For example, put empty spirals in a neat pile with the films to be developed on whichever side of the bench you prefer; when they are loaded, move the spirals to the other side of your work bench. Once again, remember to keep them in a neat pile, and when putting the films into developer check that all of them have gone in.

Different darkrooms have different methods of working, but this method suits us, and it is basically all that is needed to produce good negatives. We load our spirals on to a rod. Each rod will take four to five films and they are then placed in the developer. During the developing period we give agitation at the beginning for five to eight seconds. Then we repeat this agitation every three minutes during development, for the same period of time.

Once you have produced good quality negatives, unmarked and without scratching, then comes the drying. Care should be taken here when wiping down films after washing. Make sure you get all the surface water off. I find a soft chamois leather is best for this (after the film has been run through a wetting agent), but make sure that there are no particles of grit on the film before wiping down. Sometimes we need films dried in seconds and for this we put the films through methylated spirit, making sure that the film is wiped dry in seconds after immersion in the spirit. The film should then go either into a drying cabinet that is dust free or just hung on a clean line. Drying can be aided by a hair dryer provided it is not held too close. Once dry, the negatives are cut into lengths that suit the contact frame or whatever method you use for producing contact prints. The film should be put into negative bags immediately and not left lying around. Contact sheets should always be of good quality and readable.

Many a time a photograph has been missed when a photographer has remained on the assignment and sent material back to his offices for processing. A bad sheet of contacts is produced that are unreadable because they are either too washy or too dark. This happened to me on one occasion while in Vietnam. My films arrived in the *Daily Express* office and were rushed through. Contacts arrived on the picture desk but the most spectacular picture, of shells coming out of the ends of gun barrels, was missed because the contacts were very dark. Luckily a photographer colleague with a keen eye spotted this the next day, and he had one frame printed up which made a half page in the newspaper.

It seems strange that so many photographers and darkrooms go wrong with their contact prints. This is the simplest part of all photography. A schoolboy with an hour's training should be able to do this and produce ones of good quality. Aided with good, readable contacts the picture editor should be able to get a good idea of the story that he will show the editor at conference.

A photographer should also be able to see the quality of his pictures – whether they are sharp, if the subject's eyes are open and so on. He can also edit and mark the exact areas to be printed, or the parts of the negative that will need printing up to give the desired effects. At the same time he will know with confidence how many pictures are worth printing. Usually, if a photographer picks out lots of photographs for printing, the story has not stood up photographically. In desperation he tries to produce pictures out of nothing by over-selecting and printing up far too many, most of which have little chance of making the newspaper.

Contact sheets provide a good method of reliable filing, providing one has made sure that adequate caption details and dates are on them; unfortunately a photographer on a newspaper or magazine is more often than not in somebody else's hands when it comes to his photographs being selected for printing. There are also people who find it difficult to read contact sheets and photographers who give inadequate captions, so always remember: while on an assignment give full captions and at the same time give details or any special instructions for the picture desk and darkroom about particular photographs.

I have already emphasised that negatives must not be left lying around the darkroom while awaiting printing, for it is while handling the film that many people put sticky fingers on the emulsion of the film surface, or lay them down on surfaces that are dusty or rough. How many great photographs have been damaged in this way I dread to think. A rule always to remember here: handle negatives only by the edges and work on a spotlessly clean surface. It will save much frustration later while printing.

Now we come to the printing stage. Let us make no mistake about this, printing is a skilled job. I don't believe any automatic printing machine is a challenge to any man.

When the printer receives negatives and contact sheets marked up and ready for printing, he will take the strip of negative with the ones required, examine it for dust and look at the quality of the negative before putting it into the enlarger. The best way to spot dust particles is to hold it under the enlarging lens in the white light that is projected down, tilting it from side to side. Any dust should be removed with the aid of a soft brush or by simply blowing on the surface. It goes without saying that the enlarger and the condenser lenses should all be perfectly clean, as well as the negative carrier, for it is pointless having dirty condenser lenses and a dirty enlarger which will only put more dust on to the film.

You are now at the stage of doing your first print. The negative is in the enlarger and you pull the image up to the required size while the enlarging lens is still at full aperture, making sure that the projected image is sharp, then you stop the lens down, maybe two or three stops. This helps to give sharper definition over all the photograph and to control the amount of light falling on the sensitive printing paper. At this time the printer will decide on the grade of paper that will best suit the negative. A good average negative should print on Grade 2. If the negative is thin it will go on a harder grade, for example, Grade 3. If it is a contrasty negative a softer grade of paper is vital, for selecting the wrong grade will give uninspiring flat or contrasting prints. Some photographers use the printing in such a way as to heighten the impact – I do myself on occasions – but on the whole newspapers like a good quality print with detail. Very contrasting or flat prints are unacceptable in the average newspaper or magazine, though glossy fashion magazines might think they are works of art.

The most important thing to try for is a good quality print. Once you have selected the grade of paper, make your test print. Here is where experience tells, shading the areas that need holding back or printing up the other parts of the picture, making a mental note of the exposure time given to the print. The print, once in the developer, appears in a short while. Too fast and it will go dark; too slow in developing under the red light, and it will fail and go flat. Then there are other points to decide. When to put the print in the fixer? Does it need more exposure or less? But all this is best learnt by practical experience.

No matter what sort of quality your first print is, it is still worth turning the white light on to see if it is sharp. You can tell this by the grain; examine it for any dust marks. There might also be lines across the picture, caused by either scratching while in the film cassette or camera, or while wiping the film down. These scratches can sometimes be removed quite easily. Take the negative out, rub your little finger on your forehead to get some natural grease, and gently rub it into the emulsion or onto the back of the film, filling in the scratch. I learned this trick years ago while working as a developer boy at Keystone with probably one of the greatest printers of all times, Tom Bunt. He would do it on the old glass negatives and cut sheet films used in those days. It worked wonders and still does today with miniature films.

Sometimes we get overexposed films. We describe these as thick – in other words, very dense and nigh impossible to print. It also means exposing the print for a long period of time. To get over this we sometimes use ferric cyanide to reduce the density of the negative. Care and a few experiments should be carried out before attempting this on a very valued negative. For very thin negatives use an intensifier, which will give you more density in the negative. Still, if you have taken care in the early stages you won't have these problems, but if you do have to resort to these treatments be careful.

Now for the final print. The image of the perfect print to me is something very exciting, it is something I never get bored with. Is the expression of the subject right? Is the picture photographically interesting? Has my assignment been a complete waste of time? One is never 100% sure until the image appears through the developer.

I will leave the real art of printing of your photographs to be gained by experience. At the same time, I hope you have taken in my advice about producing good negatives. If you have, then printing will be that much easier.

128. Freddie Laker

I took this photograph when Freddie Laker (now Sir Freddie) was still trying to get permission to fly his Skytrain across the Atlantic. Wanting to get something different I told his publicity department about my idea of taking a row of aircraft seats onto the runway at Gatwick airport and having Freddie Laker sit in one. My colleague Paul Sargent immediately came up with a good caption title: 'F for Freddie, L for Laker, waiting to take-off on Runway One at Gatwick Airport'. It summed up all Mr Laker's frustration over the fights he had had with both British and American governments to get permission to operate cheap fare flights.

It is always that something different in a picture such as this that makes a newspaper give it good space; this one was splashed right across one page. It was taken on a 105mm lens on my 35mm camera at a speed of 1/250 second at f8.

129. Making Friends

The picture of Kenneth More was taken on location in Austria during a break in the filming of 'The Slipper and The Rose'.

Taken on a 35mm camera with a 28mm lens, the aperture was f16, at a speed of 1/125 second on Tri X film. Photographically, the picture was not helped by the high mid-day sun casting deep shadows around the face and a hard contrasting light in other areas. I used a three-times filter to give some lift to the clouds and the background. A flash could have been used to fill in the shadows, but I decided against this as I felt it would lose some of the spontaneity of this little local girl making friends with a famous international film star.

130

130. Charlotte Rampling on Location

A picture taken on location in southern Ireland. As usual on film sets the photographer must be patient in waiting for those few seconds when the star is available during a lull in filming. For these precious moments I always make sure I'm set up and know exactly what I want and how I will photograph my subject, looking beforehand for interesting and uncluttered backgrounds.

For these pictures I bracket my exposures both in colour and black and white, i.e. 1/30 second at f11 and f16 for colour, and 1/60 second and at f11 and 16 for the black and white, using a three-times yellow filter. The flash was some two yards away from the camera (a similar arrangement to the pictures of the young couple that I mentioned in Chapter 2). Depending on the type of effect I'm trying to achieve I would vary the distance of flash from subject, either bouncing light into a white umbrella or firing the flash direct at the subject, also through the umbrella, being careful not to over-flash. The picture was helped considerably by printing up the background and holding back the hand and face by shading. I slightly under-develop black and white films when exposing like this to avoid unnecessary contrast between subject and foreground. Of course I have a failure rate when photographing with this sort of set up, but a perfect negative should be achieved in about six exposures.

131. Jean Seberg

I first photographed the late Jean Seberg, then a very young Canadian girl, in the mid-fifties during the filming of Otto Preminger's 'Joan of Arc' in which she starred. It was in Paris recently while she was producing her own film that I photographed her again. I find it strange how the mind retains a photographic image of people and places, perhaps because we think photographically and freeze the subject for that one instant. Miss Seberg had of course grown up over the years into a mature, attractive woman who had made many films since I first photographed her. No longer was she just a young actress; she was now making her own film and that was exactly what I wanted to capture in this photograph.

The 135mm lens was ideal as it allowed me to be unobtrusive while picture-taking; the 35mm camera was loaded with Tri X film, the exposure 1/250 second at f8.

Index